Applied
Lending Techniques

2nd Edition

Applied
Lending Techniques

2nd Edition

C. N. Rouse FCIB

LES50NS
Financial Publishing

Lessons Financial Publishing Limited
Fitzroy House
11 Chenies Street
London WC1E 7ET
United Kingdom

Email: fwpeditorial@fiftylessons.com

Typeset by John Smith
Printed by Alden Press

© LES5ONS Publishing Limited 2005

First published by the Chartered Institute of Bankers 1992
Reprinted 1993, 1994, 1998, 2005

ISBN 0-85297-537-6

Contents

Foreword   vii

1   Introduction   1

2   Personal customers   11

3   Working capital proposals   23

4   Capital expenditure proposals   55

5   Speculative builders   79

6   Property lending   95

7   Professionals   109

8   Retailers   125

9   Restaurants   147

10 Farmers   167

11 Trade finance   183

12 Acquisition finance   199

13 Clubs and associations   229

Index   241

Acknowledgements

I am indebted to Lester Firkins, David Heard, Stephen Mostyn and Malcolm Unwin for supplying some of the case material; to Bryan Hayter, Lester Firkins and Stuart Croot for helping to knock it into shape; and to Fiona Somverville for her work over a hot typewriter.

Dedication

To Carol, Sophie and William

Foreword

I have been Chief Examiner for The Chartered Institute of Banker's examinations that include lending for the 11 years between 1988 and 1998. In that time I estimate that I have set 132 questions. These questions were all drawn from real-life situations. It is in fact very difficult to create artificial lending situations, and it has been my good fortune to have spent a large portion of my recent career in credit functions in different parts of the Barclays Group. This has provided me with a large body of lending case material, to which must be added my thanks to those people who have sent me interesting cases from their own lending portfolios.

My own recent experience of lending includes a spell in Barclays' Central Advances Department dealing with some of the bank's biggest advances, a period as Risk Management Director in Barclays' City Corporate Group looking after the complexities of the sort of specialist businesses one finds in the City of London and, more recently, as Group Risk Director of Barclays' Mercantile Business Finance, Barclays' leasing and hire purchase business.

Currently I am Corporate Director of Barclays Bank of Kenya handling, amongst other things, the different challenges of lending in a Third World country. I think that I can fairly say that my experience as a lender has been as varied as anyone I know.

Lending is a practical subject that, on the one hand, requires the practitioner to have a good theoretical knowledge and, on the other, to be 'street wise' in using it. The theoretical techniques can be learned from books, but usually becoming 'street wise' requires real experience. This book aims to beat this accepted wisdom by using 'real-life' cases to teach the practical side of lending.

Not all the views expressed will find favour with all bankers. Scattered amongst the accepted lending concepts are ideas of my own. I have certainly made plenty of mistakes during my career, and I have lost more money than I would ideally have wished. But declining deals produces no profits, and finding ways of doing business is an important attribute in the skilled lender. The axiom must be to be risk aware and not risk averse. The cases here tend to be marginal propositions, and so there can be more than one valid answer. While some people will disagree with my approach and decisions, all I can say is that they have worked for me.

CN Rouse
Nairobi
February 1999

Introduction

My previous publication for The Chartered Institute of Bankers, *Bankers' Lending Techniques*, had the aim of interpreting lending theory in a practical way. Ideally, a number of case studies would have been included to show how the various lending techniques might be applied, but lack of time and space prevented this. This book is intended to remedy that omission, and will attempt to show how lending techniques can be applied to practical examples.

I have been the Chief Examiner for The Chartered Institute of Bankers' main lending papers for 11 years. In producing examination questions in that time I have looked at a wealth of case-study material. The best examination questions are based on real-life cases where the decision to lend or not is marginal. Such cases illustrate most clearly the dilemmas that bankers face, and are therefore very useful potential teaching aids.

British banks are currently being subjected to severe criticism for not supporting small businesses. At the same time they are experiencing some of the largest bad debt provisions in their history. Where is the correct balance that results in a prudent lending decision as opposed to one that is risk adverse to the point of being too cautious? I am of the school that believes banking to be an art and not a science.

This means that while there are many helpful formulae and techniques, they have to be applied with judgement and common sense. This is where a banker's true skill lies. And it is not so difficult. The main requirement is to assess the evidence provided as part of any banking proposition in a dispassionate and logical way. Preconceptions that can skew a lending decision have to be avoided and the facts allowed to speak for themselves.

Bankers' Lending Techniques sets out the tools of analysis that lenders need. The present book draws heavily upon those tools. I strongly recommend students of banking to read it before embarking on this book, as they will find the background it gives invaluable in dealing with the case studies that appear later. While not wishing to repeat the whole of *Bankers' Lending Techniques* here, it is appropriate to highlight briefly some of its most salient points.

The professional approach

Bankers need to approach lending propositions with healthy scepticism. Banks do not have to do business with people they feel uncomfortable with. A 'gut reaction' feeling of unease should always be taken very seriously. Not all customers, or their professional advisors, are scrupulously honest. Many see banks as 'fair game', while others may be so determined, or at worst desperate, to raise funds that they will simply present a case to get what they want.

Approaches for borrowing from customers of other banks merit special caution. No bank likes to lose good customers, so why is the approach being made at all?

The overriding need is to form an objective view. This means not being influenced by outside pressures or preconceptions. While every lender would wish to be regarded as 'professional' by customers, this must not lead to taking decisions too quickly or on the basis of inadequate information. It is the bank that is being asked to assume the risk, so it is entitled to be given sufficient time and information to understand and evaluate a proposition. Reaching the wrong decision is hardly professional! Any lending proposition is a combination of facts, projections/estimates and opinions. These elements have to carry a different weight in the evaluation process, and at all times it will be necessary to look for evidence that will provide independent corroboration of what a customer is saying. While it may be necessary on occasions to make some assumptions, these need to be well informed and based on commonsense reasoning.

Historical financial accounts

The analysis of historical financial accounts is probably the most widely used lending technique. Many books have been published on how to make the best use of them. In many instances they will be the prime source of factual data on a business. However, this is not to say that audited accounts represent gospel truth, and as the case study at the end of this chapter shows, there are a number of ways of manipulating accounts to make them show a more rosy picture than is actually the case. The shortcomings of historical financial accounts are wellknown. The main problem areas are:

(a) The figures are historical and relate to the past rather than the future. Performance in the past is no guarantee of performance in the future, although it is often very comforting to know that a track record of success does exist.

(b) The accounts are always out of date. Particularly where small businesses are concerned, it is not unusual to find a balance sheet more than 12 months overdue, so that the situation it describes may have no relevance to the current position.

(c) The balance sheet is a snapshot of the business at one point in time. This gives plenty of opportunity for 'window dressing', and for many businesses the relationship between the various assets and liabilities as at the date of the audited accounts is very different from that during other parts of the year.

(d) The balance sheet will show only assets and liabilities that can be measured in financial terms. There will be many other non-financial assets and liabilities that need to be considered when thinking about the viability of a business, such as the quality of the management, or the workforce.

(e) The main aim in the production of the accounts is to minimize tax. In fact, I suspect that most finance directors of companies see this as being their prime duty, often to the detriment of other important tasks in the running of the business. The easiest way of minimizing tax is by manipulating the stock figure. In most cases, this is shown in the accounts of directors' valuation, and the figure is accepted by the auditor without an independent check. This kind of situation is a fact of life for most bank managers, and it is unhelpful to suggest that all financial accounts should be taken at face value. It will be the true position that a banker is interested in, although discovering it may involve a great deal of hard work and probing.

Management accounts

Management accounts are different from financial accounts in that their main aim is to supply the management of a business with current information on the immediate past and make projections for the future. They are therefore much more up to date, and ought to be more user-friendly for the purpose of monitoring and controlling the progress of a business.

Lenders will often be supplied with management accounts so that they can monitor progress in the immediate past, and almost always with a new lending proposition there will be a financial plan for the future in the form of a budget and cash flow forecast.

When a business is committed to formal planning and does it well, management accounts and projections can be a very useful tool to the lender. However, probably only a minority of businesses fall into this category, and a large proportion of the management accounts and projections seen by bankers are put forward to produce a given end result. When a borrowing is requested, the associated cash flow forecast will tend to show that it is needed and that it can be repaid within a reasonable time.

It is not unreasonable for a lender to treat with suspicion cash flow forecasts and budgets that have been prepared by or at the request of businesses that would not usually undertake any formal financial planning. Sales forecasts in such projections are often over-optimistic, and a lender cannot expect outside accountants to curb the optimism of their clients. There is a real danger in insisting on detailed projections or relying on management accounts from unsophisticated small business customers. It can be difficult to decline a proposition, even though it might look generally unsound, when faced with a budget and/or cash flow forecasts that mathematically indicate otherwise. It will very often be difficult to test the assumptions behind the figures. For example, the sales assumptions will be of critical importance, but more often than not the customer's word that they are realistic has to be accepted.

It is prudent to be especially sceptical of forecasts that are significantly different from recent actual performance unless good reasons for the prospective improvement are advanced. The evidence provided by a sound track record is always the key to deciding whether future projections are achievable or not.

Security generally gets a bad press in most textbooks, and in my opinion is not given the weight in theory that most lenders will recognize it has in practice. I am sceptical of the argument that says that a banker should lend against security only when he or she is also prepared to lend unsecured. This defies common sense.

However, it is important to understand what security is. It is alternative repayment. In most lending propositions there will be a primary source of repayment – in the case of a business, from cash flow generated by trading – and if this holds up, there will be no problem. However, things can go wrong, trading conditions can deteriorate, and the business can fail. In such an instance, repayment to the business's creditors will have to come from asset realizations. If a lender can achieve preferential treatment by taking security, then he or she would be foolish not to do so.

The extent of the risk of the primary sources of repayment failing will determine the extent to which the security is relied on: if a heavy reliance is being placed on it the lender will have to be very careful in establishing the value of the assets.

Being fully secured is not being once-times covered by the value of the asset. In a liquidation, asset values will not hold up, and it is the eventual sale proceeds of the asset that will be available to repay the borrowing. A security margin will be needed to cover:

(a)   any fall in value between the date of the advance and the sale of the asset;

(b)   the costs of sale and other necessary costs relating to the need to keep the asset saleable, such as security, insurance and maintenance costs on the property;

(c)   the roll-up of interest since the last charging date.

For a lender to be fully secured, the security margin should include a reasonable estimate of the effect of these elements on the security value, and an appropriate margin should be specified.

Case

Tootsies Limited was established eight years ago by two brothers, Mark and Oliver Toe, who are now aged 43 and 39 years. The company manufactures hosiery (socks and ladies' stockings and tights). However, nine months ago the sock division was sold.

The company currently banks with one of your competitors. The directors call to see you today, bringing their latest audited accounts and a cash flow projection for the next calendar year (see below). They have requested increased facilities from their present bank but have been refused, and they ask if you would agree the following limits:

		£
(a)	Loan to take over present borrowing	75,000
(b)	Loan to carry out essential repairs to factory	12,000
(c)	Overdraft for working capital	38,000
		125,000

As security, they offer a debenture over the assets of the company and unlimited personal guarantees supported by second mortgages over their houses (M. Toe: house value £60,000, first mortgage £40,000; O. Toe: house value £85,000, first mortgage £40,000).

In the course of your discussion with the Toe brothers, you learn the following:

(a)   The business premises were bought five years ago with the help of a bank loan. This purchase, together with subsequent spending on machinery, has placed a strain on liquidity.

(b)   In August Year B, the company's overdraft limit was removed and the balance transferred to loan account. Since then cheques have been returned unpaid.

(c)   Although the requested overdraft facility of £38,000 is well in excess of the maximum requirement shown in the cash flow, it is needed in order to take advantage of exceptional discounts of up to 20% that have just become available from suppliers of materials.

(d)   The sock division, which the Toes say was making losses, was sold nine months ago to a cousin of theirs for £40,000. (The sale amount appears in the Year B accounts under 'other debtors'.) This sale will produce a saving in wages of £21,000 in a full year against a loss of only £60,000 of sales.

You ask the Toes for time to consider their request.

This proposition represents the not unusual situation of a customer of another bank being 'misunderstood' and wanting to transfer the account.

TOOTSIES LIMITED
BALANCE SHEETS

| As at 31 July | Year A | | Year B | |
Current assets	£	£	£	£
Cash	1,450		1,236	
Debtors – trade	33,879		36,113	
– other	2,625		42,420	
Stock	143,670	181,624	145,118	224,887
Current liabilities				
Creditors	114, 167		145,306	
Hire purchase	12,695		7,523	
Bank overdraft	60,475		50,799	
Directors' loans	5,455		5,455	
Tax	–	192,792	300	209,383
Net current assets		(11,168)		15,504
Bank loan		(37,000)		(35,000)
Fixed assets				
Freehold property	70,181		118,000	
Plant and machinery	61,200	131,381	56,819	174,819
Net assets		83,213		155,323
Financed by:				
Ordinary shares		30,000		30,000
Capital reserve		–		47,819
Profit and loss account		53,213		77,504
		83,213		155,323

PROFIT AND LOSS SUMMARY

12 months to 31 July	Year A £	Year B £
Sales	488,687	457,079
Gross profit	85,142	78,939
Profit before tax (*after* extraordinary items)	2,080	24,591
Extraordinary profit on sale of sock division	–	32,000

CASH FLOW FORECAST (YEAR C)

	January	February	March	April	May	June	July	August	September	October	November	December
No. of weeks	(5)	(4)	(4)	(4)	(5)	(4)	(4)	(4)	(5)	(4)	(4)	(4)
	£	£	£	£	£	£	£	£	£	£	£	£
Sales ledger	36,000	36,000	36,000	36,000	36,000	36,000	36,000	20,000	25,000	36,000	36,000	36,000
VAT	1,700	1,700	1,700	1,700	1,700	1,700	1,700	1,700	1,700	1,700	1,700	1,700
	37,700	37,700	37,700	37,700	37,700	37,700	37,700	21,700	26,700	37,700	37,700	37,700
Wages and PAYE (incl. directors)	7,000	7,000	7,000	7,000	7,000	7,000	7,000	7,000	7,000	7,000	7,000	7,000
General overheads	2,500	2,500	2,500	2,500	2,500	2,500	2,500	2,500	2,500	2,500	2,500	2,500
Materials	23,000	23,000	23,000	23,000	23,000	19,000	19,000	19,000	19,000	19,000	19,000	19,000
Rates/property tax	375	375	375	375	375	375	375	375	375	375	375	375
Hire purchase	390	390	390	390	390	390	390	390	390	390	390	390
Pension/life assurance	360	360	360	360	360	360	360	360	360	360	360	360
Insurance	750	750	750	750	750	750	750	750	750	750	750	750
Bank loan	1,200	1,200	1,200	1,200	1,200	1,200	1,200	1,200	1,200	1,200	1,200	1,200
	35,575	35,575	35,575	35,575	35,575	31,575	31,575	31,575	31,575	31,575	31,575	31,575
Opening bank balance	(15,000)	(12,875)	(10,750)	(8,625)	(6,500)	(4,375)	1,750	7,875	(2,000)	(6,875)	(750)	5,375
Closing bank balance	(12,875)	(10,750)	(8,625)	(6,500)	(4,375)	1,750	7,875	(2,000)	(6,875)	(750)	5,375	11,500

There are quite a few warning signs, even before an analysis of the historical accounts is carried out. Although the business has been established for some time and must have performed adequately in the past, it looks as though the directors have already been given more than one chance by their present bank. The company's overdraft has only recently been funded to loan account, which must have represented an attempt by the present bank to exercise tighter control. The subsequent need to dishonour cheques shows that whatever was agreed between the Toes and their bank has not been adhered to. This must be a major warning sign, as there is no point doing business with people who cannot keep their word.

While, ideally, three years' audited accounts should always be seen, the two years we have are quite revealing if looked at with a degree of healthy scepticism. The Year B accounts look as though they have been 'window dressed'. The improvement between Year A and Year B is due to a revaluation of the company's freehold – on what basis? – and an exceptional profit of £32,000 on the sale of the sock division to a relative! This sale does not appear to be at arm's length, and needs to be treated with extreme caution. The fact is that the sock division has not actually been paid for at the time of the Year B accounts, so in practical terms has the disposal actually happened? Until cash is handed over, the sale cannot be firm. Quite why someone should want to pay £40,000 for the sale of a division that was making losses is not apparent. But the inclusion of an exceptional debtor of £40,000 relating to the sale has helped transform a lot of the balance sheet ratios. The current ratio and acid test are improved, and the inclusion of the £32,000 exceptional profits and the property revaluation in net tangible assets has greatly improved gearing.

The gross margin is holding steady, but the actual trend in net profit is down. Excluding the extraordinary profit in Year B, the trading performance in that year is actually a loss of £7,409.

Against this background, the projections for the future are simply a story that is difficult to test. The overall projected sales performance of £405,000 does not seem unreasonable against the historic figures, but the projections are crude, with the same level of sales for both four- and five-week months. While the overall suggested performance does not seem impossible to achieve, the recent poor actual performance does not augur well.

Given the overall need for caution, what security would be available? While the deeds have recently been revalued, the fact that essential repairs to the factory are said to be

RATIOS AND LOSS SUMMARY

	31 July Year A £	31 July Year B £
Current ratio	0.94:1	1.19:1
Acid test	0.20:1	0.38:1
Credit given (days)	25	29
Credit taken (days)	143	209
Stock turnover (days)	130	140
Gross profit margin (%)	17.4	17.2
Net profit margin (%)	0.4	–
Interest cover (times)	1.1	0.4
Net gearing (directors' loans as capital) (%)	123	57

necessary makes it sound as if this is an older property for which there might be a limited market. In a break-up, the deeds would not realize £118,000 and would be more likely to raise around 60% of book value, say £70,000. Even if debtors raise 70% of book value – £25,000 – stock would produce very little. Taking second charges over matrimonial homes in a situation like this is asking for trouble, and the second charges certainly could not be relied on.

With thin security cover and an apparent deliberate attempt to misrepresent the state of the business in the accounts, the Toes do not look like people a bank should trust.

2

Personal customers

There are fundamentally only two types of personal borrowing proposition:

(a) *bridging facilities* – overdrafts and bridging loans;

(b) *term repayment facilities* – repayment loans of various types, including mortgages.

Overdrafts and bridging loans have been placed together because they arise either from a need for funds pending the arrival of a specific receipt or as a general 'in case of need' arrangement, which allows a formalized borrowing arrangement in anticipation of receipt of income.

Loans that are repayable over a term can in turn be seen to fall into three categories:

(a) personal loans;

(b) house mortgages;

(c) other loans.

It is now almost universally the case that personal loans are assessed using credit-scoring techniques. Credit scoring is a statistical method of assessment that works by picking out characteristics that, based on the lender's experience, are likely to apply to a suitable applicant. Each piece of information on the application form is given a score: if the total of these scores is above a set 'pass mark', the loan will probably be approved. This technique does not involve the need for judgement by a lender, and therefore does not fall within the scope of this book. The evaluation of personal loans *per se* will not be dealt with here, but much of the information on mortgages and other loans will also apply to a judgemental credit evaluation of a personal loan that was not credit scored.

Personal financial philosophy

Every individual has a personal financial philosophy that affects their borrowing decisions and their capacity to repay. Such a philosophy will rarely be formalized, but may be characterized as the degree of pessimism or optimism with which a customer will approach the borrowing of money and its repayment.

In broad terms there are two main types of borrower (that is not to deny that there are shades of grey in between, but in general most customers can be put into one of the two groups). The first type is a person who is financially conservative and does not really feel comfortable borrowing at all. He or she leaves plenty of margin for error, is risk averse, and lives within his or her means. He or she will avoid paying charges on an overdrawn bank account, and the cheque account will run with credit balances and in a trouble-free manner. This is the sort of borrower we all want to lend to.

The second type of borrower is a person who feels entitled to a particular standard of living. This person says to him or herself: 'I work hard, so I am going to have the things I want now'. This kind of customer 'takes the waiting out of wanting', and will spend on impulse without fully calculating the consequences. Risks in borrowing will be taken, and such individuals are prepared to be optimistic about repayment prospects. In extreme cases such a borrower does not think about the consequences of borrowing at all and rapidly runs into problems. This broad type of borrower is an over-spenders and has a cheque account that is regularly overdrawn and/or frequently in excess of whatever limit is agreed.

While the first type of borrower represents a lender's ideal personal customer, in the nature of things lenders spend most time dealing with the second type. The first type of borrower really does the lender's job for him: he or she carries out a kind of credit self-assessment, based on standards probably higher than the lender would apply. The second category is the one which requires the most skill on the part of the lender, and it is in dealing with the kind of lending proposition they present that the lender's skill is tested.

Case 1

....

Charles Monday is marketing director of a small public company that banks with you. He is 38 years old, married with two sons aged 7 and 9. His current income is £40,000 per annum. When Monday took up his present job two years ago he moved his account to your branch. At that time he purchased a new house for £120,000 and, as an exceptional matter in view of the connection, you granted him a mortgage of £80,000, which included the consolidation of a £7,500 overdraft he had run up at his previous bank. You agreed this arrangement partly because he had received a large salary increase on starting the new job and on the basis that he kept his account in credit in future. Subsequently you agreed an overdraft limit of £2,000 to cover delays in receipt of his business expenses.

Monday's overdraft has been showing a steadily increasing trend, and just before his last month's salary was received it stood at £3,600. You now receive a status enquiry on Monday that appears to relate to a Gold Card overdraft limit at another bank, one of your competitors. You telephone Monday and ask him to call to see you to discuss matters.

At your meeting Monday tells you he has applied for a £10,000 Gold Card overdraft limit at the other bank because he needs some leeway to meet school fees of £700 per term for his younger son, who will shortly be joining his brother at a private school. In addition to this, Monday tells you that he and his wife have run up debts on various credit cards over the past two years totalling £3,000. His job is going well and he hopes to receive a 10% salary increase in the near future, but in view of his previous arrangement to keep his account in credit he feels that you would be unsympathetic to a request for increased facilities.

However, as he has banked with you for nearly two years, he would prefer to confine his borrowing to your bank. Monday therefore asks whether you would be prepared to increase his overdraft to £10,000 although he would prefer to top up his mortgage, ideally by £15,000. He believes his house is now worth £180,000.

Before the meeting, you carried out a brief check on Monday's account, that revealed:

    (a)   His net monthly salary is just over £2,000.

    (b)   Regular monthly payments: mortgage £835, community rates/tax £100.

    (c)   Overdraft interest for the last quarter amounted to £85.

This is a difficult request to deal with because Mr Monday is the kind of personal customer a bank wants – he is a high earner with useful connections and in a good job. However, he most definitely falls into the second category of borrower. Despite his good income, he regularly spends more than he earns, as evidenced by both the increasing overdraft and the credit card debts. He has an expensive lifestyle and must be a constant nuisance to the bank, with regular appearances on the morning computer print-out and so on. He is the sort of customer who has debts that he does not tell the bank about, and despite having been 'sorted out' once, he is back in trouble again. His attitude appears to be essentially one of short-term expediency, and it may be that he has no real intention of cutting back his expenditure, although this is the only way in that the increased borrowing can be repaid.

- If his proposal is accepted, the bank will probably have an overdraft that would not fluctuate or be repaid or, alternatively, a mortgage where repayments could only be financed at the expense of a new overdraft.

- The amount Monday has asked for – either £10,000 or £15,000 – would give him some leeway to continue his excess expenditure in the short term. But if he is unwilling to do anything about his expenditure – and with a young family this is not going to be reduced easily – he will eventually put himself in the position where he will have to 'trade down' houses to repay his debts.

- There is probably sufficient equity in the house to ensure that the bank would not be on risk in lending more, so I suspect that in most instances Monday would find a lender to do what he wants. However, the only long-term solution is for Monday to produce a realistic expenditure budget and stick to it. I rather suspect that he would not be able to do this, given his particular personal financial philosophy, but no doubt his banker will 'grin and bear it' and take good margins and commission income on the account.

Case 2

Anthony Murray has banked with you for three years and has maintained a generally satisfactory account. His balances have never been large and regular overdrafts have been seen, but always within the internal limit you mark on his account.

Murray calls to see you. He is a foreman at a local engineering company. He has been offered another job in a nearby town at an increased salary of £21,000 per annum. His wife currently works part-time in a supermarket earning £50 per week. The journey to the new job would be difficult from his present house and he wishes to move.

His present house has been valued by a local estate agent at £65,000, and there is a mortgage to a building society of £40,000. Mr and Mrs Murray have seen a house they want to buy. The asking price is £72,000 and the building society has agreed a mortgage of £52,000. Mr Murray would like to move as quickly as possible.

Mr Murray is a well-established customer, and his request for a bridging loan is one that has to be taken seriously. However, from the run of his account it appears that he falls into the second category of borrower. It needs to be recognized that he may tend to be optimistic, and his judgement may be swayed by the prospect of getting what he wants as soon as possible.

The request is basically for an open-ended bridging loan, and in *Bankers' Lending Techniques* I set out some rules of thumb to be applied to this type of lending. To summarize these briefly, an open-ended bridging loan should only be undertaken when:

(a)   the housing market is buoyant;

(b)   an early sale of the existing property is in prospect;

(c)   there is sufficient margin in the transaction to allow for a 20% reduction in price and interest roll-up for a year.

The current state of the housing market will be a matter for the judgement of the lender at the time, and while we have no information on the sale prospects of Murray's present house, some simple enquiries should establish this. How then do the figures look?

	£
Purchase price	72,000
Less: New mortgage	52,000
	20,000
Plus: To clear present mortgage	40,000
Loan needed	60,000

To be repaid by:	£
Sale proceeds of present house	65,000
Margin	5,000

The margin is too small even before the various costs of moving, that will probably be around £3,000, are taken into account. So a prudent lender would decline to provide an open-ended bridging loan.

One way forward in this kind of situation is to consider whether a bigger mortgage could be provided on the new property to widen the margin. In this instance, with Murray's wife apparently going to lose her income in the short term and given the past history of the account, this would not appear appropriate. The lender would do Murray no favours in allowing him to overstretch himself.

There should be no problems in providing a closed bridging loan for, say, a 10% deposit of £7,200 once contracts for the sale of the present property have been exchanged.

Case 3

Roger Mason has maintained an account with you for over 20 years. He is a company director who is due to retire in 12 months' time. In anticipation of his retirement, he wishes to buy a house by the sea while retaining a flat in town. Mr and Mrs Mason have seen a house they want to buy in a seaside resort, together with a flat they like. The house will cost £150,000 and the flat £95,000. Their present house has been valued at £270,000 free of mortgage.

Mason currently earns £50,000 per annum, and when he retires he will be able to commute his pension to produce a capital sum of £100,000 and a continuing pension of £18,000 per annum. Alternatively, he could have a pension of £30,000 per annum without commutation. Mr Mason would like to proceed with his plans as soon as possible.

Although no account information is given for Mr Mason, he has obviously made more than adequate pension arrangements to ensure a good income after his retirement, and the fact that his present house is free of mortgage suggests that he is more likely to fall into the first category of borrower than the second. He is probably not someone who would enter into a risky transaction lightly.

The same general considerations in relation to an open-ended bridging loan will apply as for Case 2. The figures look like this:

	£
Purchase price – house	150,000
– flat	95,000
Loan needed	245,000
Sale proceeds of present house	270,000
Margin	25,000

Expenses in relation to the move are likely to be high, because two properties are being purchased, and could amount to between £11,000 and £12,000. The margin to meet the 20% price reduction and interest for 12 months would have to be in the order of £86,000 and therefore is clearly insufficient. However, if Mason was to commute his pension, £100,000 would be available to meet any shortfall and/or a mortgage could be granted against one of the properties.

There would be little risk to the bank in going ahead but, as with most open-ended bridging loans, the customer would be ill-advised to put a large part of his or her personal wealth at risk unnecessarily. This is particularly the case with Mr Mason, who would be putting his retirement nest-egg on the line. He should be advised not to proceed, but if the properties are indeed ideal and he wishes to go ahead, he will undoubtedly find a lender prepared to go forward with him.

Case 4

David Keen is a salesman with a local electrical company. He is 40 years old and has banked with you for the five years he has worked for the company. His monthly salary credit varies with the amount of sales commission he earns but averages £900. You regularly allow him overdrafts on his account in anticipation of the receipt of his salary credit. The range of his account over the last 12 months has been £403 debit – £695 credit; the average balance has been £151 credit.

Mr Keen's mother died recently. Probate has just been granted. Mr Keen and his brother Paul are the executors and the sole and equal beneficiaries under Mrs Keen's will. The Keen brothers expect the estate to realize £25,000.

The brothers wish to use their inheritance to buy jointly a holiday home in Spain. They have found a property that they can acquire for £50,000 provided they can complete the purchase quickly. David Keen asks you for a loan of £25,000 over 10 years, to reduce by £12,500 when he receives his share of the inheritance. His brother is approaching his own bank with a similar proposal.

The brothers believe that they will be able to rent out the Spanish property during periods when they are not using it, thereby generating more than sufficient income to service their individual residual loans, that will total £25,000. David Keen tells you that he is prepared to grant you a mortgage over the Spanish property as security for his loan.

You question David Keen and discover that he is married with two children aged 11 and 13. His wife works part-time in a shop earning £30 per week paid in cash, and she has no bank account. Neither David Keen nor his wife has any significant savings, but they jointly own their house, that has an equity of £50,000.

This proposition falls into two distinct parts:

(a)   an initial bridging requirement of £12,500;

(b)   a ten-year repayment loan of £12,500.

The way David Keen's account has worked suggests that he falls into the second category of borrower and probably tends to over-optimism. His statements cannot be taken at face value and need to be tested. Hard evidence should be sought wherever possible.

So, in relation to the bridging requirement, Keen will need to be questioned on the liquidity of the estate to establish how quickly it can be turned into cash, and whether all the costs of realization have been taken into account in the assumed £25,000 realization figure. Ideally, some sort of confirmation from the solicitor acting should be obtained. With satisfactory assurances, the bridging requirement should be reasonably straightforward.

The repayment loan is more difficult. It is by no means clear that Keen has done his sums correctly. The amount he is seeking does not seem to be enough, as no account appears to have been taken of legal costs and so on in relation to the acquisition of the Spanish property. These will not be inconsiderable. Moreover, there will be expenses incurred, for example, for furnishing the property. How are these costs to be met?

As always, the crucial issue will be repayment. The statement that rentals will service the loan cannot be taken at face value – where is the evidence? Moreover, there will be costs in maintaining the property, and it will probably be necessary to have an agent to organize the letting, who will expect a commission. Keen must produce a formal budget setting out all income costs and so on. In other circumstances, it could be that there would be other income besides the rentals that Keen could use to support repayment. However, it is clear from the run of Keen's bank account that he has no surplus income. He is already living up to or beyond his and his wife's incomes. In fact, his own income is not of particularly good quality as part of it represents sales commission, which might disappear if, for example, he fell ill.

The suggested security arrangements are unsatisfactory, given the difficulty and uncertainty in taking a charge over a property in Spain. There would probably be sufficient security in the equity in Keen's UK property, but with the repayment proposals being at best speculative, there is too much risk.

Case 5

....

Mr Hole, one of three directors in XYZ Ltd, a firm of civil engineers, calls into your branch to tell you that he is getting divorced and requests you to increase his mortgage (that is already with your bank) so that he can 'pay off' his wife.

Your records on Mr and Mrs Hole reveal the following position:

	£
Value of property	55,000
(matrimonial home owned jointly by Mr and Mrs Hole)	
Mortgage outstanding	36,000
Salary of Mr Hole	15,000

His account over the last 12 months shows:

Best balance	803 Cr
Worst balance	964 Dr
Average balance	525 Dr

Mr Hole tells you:

(a) It has been agreed that he will pay £16,000 to his wife when the divorce is finalized.

(b) He wishes to replace several window frames and kitchen units at a cost of £8,000.

(c) The value of his property is now £75,000.

(d) His income is now £20,000 – and, as evidence of this, he hands you an extract of his firm's up-to-date profit and loss account, together with a letter from the accountants for the firm (see below).

(e) His wife works, and there are no children of the marriage.

(f) He wishes to increase the mortgage to £60,000.

Letter from Accountants:

'It would appear from discussions with the Directors that the amount of work currently being undertaken by XYZ Ltd has been increased, and the prospects for the future are good. It is understood that Mr Hole's salary is to be increased to £20,000 per annum, that in the circumstances outlined above would not appear to be unreasonable or excessive.'

Mr Hole, from the way his bank account has worked, appears to fall into the second category of borrower. However, given that he is getting divorced, it may be that his personal financial situation has been suffering from special circumstances and may not be typical of his usual personal financial philosophy. A look back at his longer-term track record might be helpful.

The income of most people requesting a loan or house mortgage is usually readily determined, and it is their ability to meet increased expenditure that is open to doubt. However, with self-employed people or, in this case, an owner-director, income payable will depend on the performance of their business. Attention needs to be given to the accounts of the business to determine how much it can afford to pay its proprietor or, in this case, proprietors. It should not be assumed that where there is

XYZ LTD
EXTRACT FROM PROFIT AND LOSS ACCOUNTS

12 months	Last year		Current year	
	£000	£000	£000	£000
Sales and work done		235		384
Cost of sales		110		201
Gross profit		125		183
Selling and distribution cost	29		51	
Establishment expenses				
(rent, rates, heat, etc.)	12		23	
Admin. expenses	37		45	
Depreciation	2	80	3	1 22
Directors' remuneration	38		44	
Pension contribution	–	38	10	54
Net profit before tax		7		7

more than one owner of a business the salary of only one can be increased without also increasing those of the others. So can this business increase directors' remuneration to £60,000? It may be possible, but more evidence of future prospects is needed.

A statement from the accountants cannot simply be taken at face value. What is the evidence?

Mr Hole also needs to complete an expenditure budget to show that he can afford the repayments, given that he has lost his wife's income. It may be that there will be a new 'partner' who may be able to share the costs.

In any event, Mr Hole does seem to be trying to do too much at once. The £8,000 for replacement of window frames and kitchen units looks a little extravagant, given that he is already taking on an increased mortgage to fund the payment to his wife. There is certainly a case for deferring the home improvements for, say, 12 months to see how he copes with a £52,000 mortgage.

A new valuation of the property will be needed but, provided this comes out near the £75,000 indicated by Mr Hole, there should be adequate security and the lender should be safe.

3

Working capital proposals

The concept of working capital

The most common type of lending by banks to businesses is for working capital purposes. In lending proposals this is generally expressed as being for 'normal trading finance' or an 'in case of need facility'.

The textbook definition of working capital is that it is the excess of current assets over current liabilities. This definition leads to semantic arguments as to whether extra bank lending can in fact provide an increase in working capital. This is because, say, a £100,000 increase in an overdraft to finance an extra £100,000 of current assets does not increase the excess of current assets over current liabilities and cannot, therefore, increase working capital on the textbook definition. The only way in which the textbook definition of working capital can be increased is through an increase in the overall net tangible assets of the business from, for example, retained profits, while keeping the amount invested in fixed assets static and/or changing fixed assets into current assets by, for example, selling property and converting it into cash.

This textbook definition of working capital is not at all helpful. The concept of working capital should be about 'oiling the wheels' of a business.

It is about the relative liquidity of different assets and liabilities and, particularly, about ensuring that a business has sufficient cash resources to meet its needs with a degree of comfort.

To give a simple example: an overdraft limit that enables a personal customer to anticipate receipt of a salary is a borrowing for working capital purposes. Meeting expenses in anticipation of receipt in the short term of known income is using an overdraft for working capital purposes. (An overdraft in anticipation of the open-ended sale of a house would not be.) The provision of such an overdraft enables the borrower to 'oil the wheels' of his personal financial arrangements. He does not have to consider the precise timing of expenditure so that it always occurs after income is to hand.

The same is true in a business. Management of a business will generally not want to delay making payments until after receipts have arrived. The provision of an overdraft allows them to concentrate on the main activity of the business and not spend time on the unproductive control of cash. This does not mean that cash planning and control is not important – in fact it is vital – but it is planning and control within broad parameters.

An overdraft that provides cash to finance assets or reduce other liabilities is an addition to the capital available to a business. It can therefore provide additional working capital. However, it is poor-quality capital from a business's point of view. It will generally be repayable on demand and will be expensive when interest rates are high. The problem with short-term borrowing as capital is that it is unstable and cannot be relied on to any great extent.

This need not be a problem if the other elements in a business are stable; but if a company is expanding quickly or hits trading difficulties, an over-reliance on short-term borrowing can be very dangerous. Lenders will face their most difficult working capital propositions when businesses are 'overtrading' or – to invent a new word – 'undertrading'. It is on dealing with these two situations that this chapter will concentrate, as they represent the most typical marginal working capital lending decisions.

Overtrading

Overtrading is characterized as an attempt by a business to carry out a level of activity with insufficient resources. The business tries to achieve a level of sales that puts a strain on its working capital resources so that there is pressure on the bank overdraft limit and delays in paying creditors. Because of the shortage of cash, there is pressure to collect debtors more quickly so that there is a temptation to give excessive discounts for quick payment.

The cure for overtrading is to provide the business with more cash, and as banks are in the business of doing this, the suggestion that overtrading is always a bad thing is a little simplistic. All bankers have lent money to companies that are overtrading. Most new companies overtrade at some stage, and the key issue is not whether to lend to overtrading businesses – it is inevitable that banks will do this – but at what level it is safe to do so.

There is a very simple answer to this. A prudent banker will agree to lend in a marginal situation, such as that represented by an overtrading business, if there is adequate security to provide an alternative source of repayment to normal trading. In practical terms, the degree of security cover available will be a key issue. As most businesses are limited companies and the major assets of an overtrading business are current assets – debtors and stock – the key will be the extent to which future borrowing can be covered by current assets picked up by debenture.

Chapter 8 of *Bankers' Lending Techniques* covers the setting of debenture formulae in some detail. The lender does not, in fact, set a debenture formula; it sets itself. It has to reflect the company's projected future assets in relation to anticipated borrowing, and will therefore be determined by the company's future budgets. The issue for the lender will be whether the budgets, and assumptions underlying them, and the consequent achievable debenture formula represent an adequate level of security cover.

Generally speaking, stock realizes very little in a break-up, and the key component of a good debenture formula will be the debtor cover element. A minimum debtor cover multiple will usually be 1½ times the liabilities to be covered. A higher multiple will be needed in those businesses where a poor level of debt recovery may be expected, such as fashion businesses or contracting.

As well as concentrating on security cover, the lender will need to be satisfied that the business's plans for the future have a good chance of success.

The appraisal of profit and cash flow forecasts is dealt with in Chapter 7 of *Bankers' Lending Techniques*. The important requirement is to test the assumptions built into the forecasts in a common-sense way and to look for hard evidence that they are achievable. The best form of hard evidence is a business's own track record, and a forecast should not seek to demonstrate a higher level of performance in what will be a more difficult environment unless there is a sound explanation.

The past movement in the amount of working capital required by a business, as evidenced by its historical statements of sources and applications of funds, can be a useful guide to future needs. However, such working capital movements need to be put into the context of the level of sales to which they relate. Additionally, as a business's future plan will usually involve the funding of part of the working capital requirement from retained profits, it is also necessary to see the extra capital that increased sales will generate internally for the business. The net working assets to sales ratio, which can be expressed as:

$$\frac{\text{Stock} + \text{Debtors} - \text{Creditors}}{\text{Sales}}$$

indicates the amount of extra capital that each extra pound of sales requires. The retentions to sales ratio, which can be expressed as:

$$\frac{\text{Retained profit}}{\text{Sales}}$$

indicates the amount of new capital that each pound of extra sales would produce.

For most businesses the figures produced by these two ratios tend to be broadly consistent over time, as they reflect the underlying nature of the business. The gap between them therefore gives a good indication of the likely extra working capital requirement that will be needed for a given increase in sales and is, therefore a useful tool to test the borrowing requirement predicted in a cash flow forecast. The practical use of these ratios is demonstrated in the cases at the end of the chapter.

Undertrading

While there are whole chapters in books about overtrading, very little is written about 'undertrading'. Undertrading may be defined as a situation where a business cannot generate sufficient cash to fund its current level of operations or a modest increase, without increased borrowing to meet working capital needs. It will mainly, but not exclusively, result from a lack of profitability. If a business makes losses, the drain of capital this represents will have to be replaced from elsewhere, and the source is likely to be short-term borrowing.

A possible alternative scenario is that an adverse change in credit terms, with creditors insisting on quicker payment and/or debtors taking longer to pay, could also require an increased working capital borrowing requirement on a static level of sales, but in practice a weakening in creditor confidence will tend to be linked to a poor profit performance.

With overtrading lending propositions there is likely to be at least some sort of recent record of success, but with undertrading propositions the lender is being asked to increase exposure against a background of recent failure.

As borrowing will be increasing and asset cover diminishing, there will also be less security available. Because something has gone wrong, remedial action will have to be taken, and the key issue will be viability of the management's plan to put things right, along with the availability of adequate security cover. When something has gone wrong, a lender will wish to have the best possible hold over a business's assets before advancing more. It is also reasonable to expect the management of the business to back their confidence in their recovery plan in a tangible way so that, for example, it will be appropriate to have directors' guarantees, perhaps supported by personal assets, if these are not already in place.

Chapter 9 of *Bankers' Lending Techniques* has a comprehensive section both on the considerations that need to be borne in mind when deciding whether to lend more, and on the sort of remedial action that businesses can take to improve their cash flow quickly. It does, however, need to be recognized that there will be situations where lending more will be 'throwing good money after bad'. It may well be better to accept a limited loss on a borrowing rather than lend more to a business that is in difficulties in the hope that things will improve. An assessment needs to be made of the lender's probable loss if more is not lent. This needs to be compared with a worst-case analysis of the potential loss in, say, six months' time, if performance continues to be poor. The extra risk has to be worth it. A lender will not be doing the customer any favours if the latter incurs more debt in pursuit of a forlorn hope. Moreover, under the terms of the Insolvency Act 1986, a director who allows a company to continue trading in circumstances where he should have concluded that there was no reasonable prospect that the company would avoid going into liquidation, may be made liable to make a contribution to the company's assets. It is important, therefore, that customers make a sensible decision.

Case 1

Banking at your branch is a company called Jack's Racks Ltd, which was established nine years ago by John Jack; John and his wife are the only shareholders and directors. The company originally manufactured metal shelving units mainly for use in warehouses. About two years ago Jack saw an opportunity to manufacture metal display cabinets for use in DIY stores and supermarkets as well. The profit margins on the display cabinets were better than on the simple shelving units.

Recent sales growth has been very fast, as the expansion of out-of-town shopping developments has meant a good demand for Jack's products. About a year ago he was able to obtain contracts from a major UK retailer, which now takes 75% of the company's production. Its workforce has increased from 20 two years ago to 150 now. Ten months ago the company moved to a new freehold factory, which you helped to finance through a £300,000 loan.

In addition to the loan you provide an overdraft facility, which you increased at the start of last year from £300,000 to £350,000, following periods when the previous limit was exceeded. Your regional office lending controller recently agreed a temporary increase in this limit to £600,000 pending the annual review, which is now due.

As security, you have a debenture giving a fixed charge over property and book debts and a floating charge over other assets. You also hold an unsupported unlimited guarantee from Jack.

Jack now calls to see you, bringing with him last year's audited accounts (Year C). Business is booming, and he expects this state of affairs to continue as his major UK retail customer has decided to refurbish its stores every three years, instead of every five as previously. He expects sales to more than double this year, with further substantial increases in the next two years. He has recruited a young accountant whom he is going to appoint financial director of the company, and together they have drawn up a three-year plan. This requires the doubling in size of the company's production facilities during the next six months, with a further significant increase next year. An increased overdraft of £750,000 is needed immediately, increasing to £1,300,000 next year.

He gives you three years' projected balance sheets and profit and loss accounts, showing the financial implications of the plan (see below).

JACK'S RACKS LIMITED
BALANCE SHEETS

As at 31 December	Year A		Year B		Year C	
	£000	£000	£000	£000	£000	£000
Current assets						
Debtors	100		169		398	
Raw materials	46		77		179	
Work in progress	148	294	309	555	1,096	1,673
Current liabilities						
Hire purchase	44		96		130	
Creditors	274		370		1,036	
Bank – overdraft	69		173		166	
– loan (current position)	–		–		5	
Tax	9	396	50	689	171	1,508
Net current assets		(102)		(134)		165
Medium-term loan		–		–		(295)
Fixed assets						
Freehold land and buildings	66		135		411	
Plant and machinery	166	232	283	418	374	785
Net assets		130		284		655
Financed by:						
Ordinary shares		3		3		3
Capital reserve		–		69		
Profit and loss account		127		212		652
		130		284		655

PROFIT AND LOSS ACCOUNT SUMMARY

12 months to 31 December	Year A	Year B	Year C
	£000	£000	£000
Sales	872	1,269	2,414
Purchases	441	604	1,438
Gross profit	300	467	1,055
Net profit before tax	104	136	551

RATIOS AND OTHER INFORMATION

12 months to 31 December	Year A	Year B	Year C
Current ratio	0.74:1	0.81:1	1.1:1
Acid test	0.25:1	0.25:1	0.26:1
Credit given (days)	34	39	30
Credit taken (days)	115	196	131
Stock turnover (days)	25	132	188
Gross margin (%)	34.4	36.8	43.7
Net margin (%)	11.9	10.8	22.8
Interest cover (times)	6.5	6.0	10.8
Net gearing (%)	87	95	91
Net working assets to sales (%)	2	15	26
Retained profits to sales (%)	7	7	18

PROJECTED FIGURES
BALANCE SHEETS

As at 31 December	Year D		Year E		Year F	
	£000	£000	£000	£000	£000	£000
Current assets						
Cash	–		–		706	
Debtors	920		1,750		2,250	
Stock	2,000	2,920	3,750	5,500	5,S00	8,456
Current liabilities						
Hire purchase	76		34			
Creditors	1,320		1,922		2,840	
Bank – overdraft	640		1,261			
– loan (current position)	7		9		11	
Tax	514	2,557	1,038	4,264	1,373	4,224
Net current assets		363		1,236		4,232
Medium-term loan		(288)		(279)		(268)
Fixed assets						
Freehold land and buildings	938		1,372		1,343	
Plant and machinery	597	1,535	1,207	2,579	1,040	2,383
Net assets		1,610		3,536		6,347
Financed by:						
Ordinary shares		3		3		3
Profit and loss account		1,607		3,533		6,344
		1,610		3,536		6,347

PROFIT AND LOSS ACCOUNT SUMMARY

12 months to 31 December	Year D	Year E	Year F
	£000	£000	£000
Sales	6,500	12,400	17,500
Purchases	2,500	4,930	7,045
Gross profit	2,195	4,123	5,763
Net profit before tax	1,469	2,964	4,325

PROJECTED BALANCE SHEET RATIOS

12 months to 31 December	Year D	Year E	Year F
Current ratio	1:1.14	1:1.29	1: 2.00
Acid test	1:0.36	1:0.41	1: 0.70
Credit given (days)	37	39	42
Credit taken (days)	172	120	123
Stock turnover (days)	139	126	144
Gross margin (%)	33.8	33.3	32.9
Net margin (%)	22.6	23.9	24.7
Interest cover (times)	12.1	17.6	81.0
Net gearing (%)	63	45	
Net working assets to sales (%)	25	29	28
Retained profits to sales (%)	15	16	16

OPERATION OF BANK ACCOUNT

	Year A £000	Year B £000	Year C £000	Year D to date £000
Average balance	31 Dr	82 Dr	123 Dr	358 Dr
Range (last 12 months):				
Year C	High		Low	
May/June	248 Dr		84 Dr	
July/August	265 Dr		138 Dr	
September/October	128 Dr		38 Dr	
November/December	303 Dr		166 Cr	
Year D to date				
January/February	421 Dr		261 Cr	
March/April	603 Dr		509 Dr	

The business is a longstanding customer that, given the position shown for Year A, can only have grown slowly. It has suddenly entered a phase of rapid expansion, and it has very ambitious plans for the next few years, which will take the company into a different size league. There must therefore be a very significant possibility of the company overtrading.

The company has a good track record, but this has been against the background of a buoyant market, and it is heavily dependent on one customer. Gearing is already high for a manufacturing business, and borrowing is projected to go higher in the immediate future. The lower projected levels of gearing will only be achieved if retained profits come through as planned. Interest cover has been good, so there is some scope to absorb an increase in interest rates, and a high level of gearing might just be sustainable if it were possible to be confident that profitability would indeed hold up in the future.

There is a significant gap between the net working assets to sales ratio and the retained profits to sales ratio. This does give an indication that the projections for reductions in borrowing may be over-optimistic. It is of concern that the business is illiquid, with a large proportion of the assets held in stock, particularly work in progress. Little credit is being given, showing that existing customers are prompt payers, but the whole situation smacks of the potential for major problems should the dominant customer insist on more credit or be unhappy with any other contracts.

Not only have retentions been insufficient to finance increased working capital needs, there also seems to be a requirement for further fixed capital expenditure. It appears that the company's intention is to fund this through short-term borrowing when it must be more prudent to seek medium-term finance. This must raise a further doubt about the feasibility of the borrowing projections.

The company's sales projections are very ambitious, with a forecast increase of five times over the next two years. Questions need to be asked about the availability of physical and management resources actually to achieve such a performance. It is fair to say that there are some relatively conservative assumptions in the lower projected gross margin and the greater credit given and lower credit taken ratios. However, in this case it is the attainment of the sales targets that must be the key to everything and which has to be most critically examined. What if the ambitious sales and profits increases do not occur? What if the business of the dominant customer is lost?

The working capital requirement would be less, but with the projections showing an extra £750,000 of fixed assets being acquired, a larger labour force presumably being necessary and overheads generally being significantly higher in the expanded premises, the fixed cost base of the business is going to be considerably higher than it is now. Failure to meet the ambitious targets is likely to leave the business in a very uncomfortable position.

Given the high risk in the proposition, would there be adequate security? The deeds of the factory should provide worthwhile cover, but there is bound to be a heavy dependence on the break-up value of the current assets. The stock is going to be largely work in progress, which may only have a scrap value; and in this instance it is likely that the debtors would also have a low realization value. The business sells on contract to a limited number of major customers. If it is unable to meet its contracts, the debtors are likely to have substantial counter-claims for breach of contract to set off against the amounts they owe on past contracts. The bank might appoint a receiver who could trade on to fulfil outstanding contracts, but this is never a very comfortable option as a receiver, inexperienced in the business, will have to succeed where the company has failed.

This is an instance where the proposed level of overtrading is just too rich for a lender – and the company will need either to find an injection of outside capital or, alternatively, to scale down its ambitious plans.

Case 2

Fatties Ltd manufactures and sells ladies' clothing in larger sizes. The company has banked with you for over 20 years. The management of the business has until recently been in the hands of the two main shareholders, Fred and Sidney Plump. Two years ago they decided to appoint a new marketing director, a Mrs Stout, as they felt that the selling of their traditional garments needed revamping. Mrs Stout has identified an expanding market for higher fashion outsize garments, particularly through mail order companies.

The company did not have the manufacturing capacity to meet any significant extra demand, and the directors decided to import the additional garments from suppliers in Hong Kong. The Hong Kong manufacturers were prepared to supply Fatties and give the company the 60-day credit terms it was seeking only on the basis that it established irrevocable documentary letters of credit to cover shipments under their contracts. The manufacturers invoice for the goods in sterling.

You are currently providing Fatties with an overdraft and/or documentary credit limit of £250,000. As security, you have a debenture giving a fixed and floating charge over the company's assets, a letter of postponement over directors' loans, and a joint and several guarantee for £50,000 from the Plumps.

The company shows its new designs to customers about six months in advance of the expected delivery of the garments.

The time is October and the company has just completed showing customers its new spring designs. There has been a high level of interest in these from mail order companies, who have placed a better-than-expected level of preliminary orders.

The directors are forecasting sales of £1.3 million for the next six months and expect to import more from Hong Kong to meet demand. They call to see you to ask for an increase in the combined facility to £450,000. They produce financial information, including management accounts in the form of projected balance sheets covering the next six months.

This case concerns a company in a fashion business seeking to expand quickly, despite a low capital base. There must therefore be a significant risk of overtrading. Moreover, not only is the company trying to borrow to fund its working capital needs, it also wants the bank to enter into documentary credit liabilities that will have the effect of guaranteeing a large proportion of the company's trade creditors. There is, therefore, considerable risk to be assessed.

Many of the typical signs of overtrading are present: liquidity is declining, in terms of both the current ratio and the acid test, while the credit taken figures show a big reduction between Years B and C, but this only reflects the change to importing a significant number of garments. Improved stock turnover also probably only reflects the switch from manufacturing to buying in stock.

The reduction in gross margin is a classic sign, with the higher sales only being achievable at lower prices. The net margin is very thin, and it is not surprising, therefore, that the retained profit to sales ratio shows that the business cannot hope to fund anything but a minuscule portion of future working capital needs from profits. The net working assets to sales ratio is in the 20-25% range – so the company can hope to fund expansion only by increased borrowing.

Gearing is high and interest cover thin for what is a high-risk business. It is the bank that is increasingly taking the strain, either directly through the overdraft or indirectly through the guarantee it is providing to trade creditors through the documentary credit arrangements.

Excesses have occurred on the bank account, and although these were temporary, there is pressure on the agreed limit. If seasonal factors (the market for clothes is essentially in the spring and the autumn as far as suppliers/manufacturers are

FATTIES LTD
BANK ACCOUNT

	Highest debit £	Lowest debit £	Average £
Year B			
October	55,641 Dr	38,527 Dr	48,872 Dr
November	68,998 Dr	40,324 Dr	58,483 Dr
December	152,161 Dr	59,770 Dr	21,206 Dr
Year C			
January	181,161 Dr	107,688 Dr	148,599 Dr
February	220,820 Dr	128,333 Dr	180,168 Dr
March	164,883 Dr	124,262 Dr	152,078 Dr
April	193,673 Dr	142,272 Dr	173,934 Dr
May	221,029 Dr	151,146 Dr	194,370 Dr
June	225,230 Dr	173,201 Dr	207,741 Dr
July	204,668 Dr	166,101 Dr	184,360 Dr
August	182,233 Dr	142,732 Dr	163,271 Dr
September	161,111 Dr	121,817 Dr	139,455 Dr

Year	Turnover £	Average balance £
Z	831,047	50,786 Dr
A	1,081,717	74,274 Dr
B	1,255,253	81,496 Dr
C to date	1,267,188	169,708 Dr

BALANCE SHEETS

As at 31 March	Year A £	Year A £	Year B £	Year B £	Year C £	Year C £	Management accounts 30 Sept. Year C £	Management accounts 30 Sept. Year C £
Current assets								
Cash	231		185		164		211	
Debtors	144,815		163,454		216,145		207,672	
Stock	233,615	378,661	234,669	398,308	298,038	514,347	311,775	519,658
Current liabilities								
Creditors	109,761		172,401		163,916		221,731	
Hire purchase	3,442		2,318		18,046		20,904	
Bank	173,253		120,554		209,887		189,912	
Directors' loans	13,369		13,470		16,414		16,414	
Current tax	330	300,135	360	309,103	14,600	422,863	14,600	463,561
Net current assets		78,526		89,205		91,484		56,097
Fixed assets								
Freehold building	53,037		53,313		58,814		73,058	
Plant and machinery	88,637	141,674	97,050	150,363	112,529	171,343	157,712	230,770
		220,200		239,568		262,827		286,867
Long-term liabilities								
Mortgage loan	18,500		18,500		18,500		18,500	
Deferred taxation	39,300	57,800	41,970	60,470	41,150	59,650	41,150	59,650
Net assets		162,400		179,098		203,177		227,217

BALANCE SHEETS *continued*

As at 31 March	Year A		Year B		Year C		Management accounts 30 Sept. Year C	
	£	£	£	£	£	£	£	£
Financed by:								
Share capital		1,000		1,000		1,000		1,000
Profit & loss account		161,400		178,098		202,177		226,217
Shareholders' funds		162,400		179,098		203,177		227,217

12 months to 31 March	Year A	Year B	Year C	6 months to 30 September
	£	£	£	£
Sales	993,520	1,242,218	1,528,531	1,009,327
Cost of goods sold	775,510	974,238	1,249,363	827,822
inc. purchases	325,308	403,835	853,984	589,887
Gross profit	218,010	267,980	279,168	181,505
Interest	10,981	16,661	18,734	13,928
Net profit before tax	38,652	24,967	37,755	24,040

PROJECTED BALANCE SHEETS

Next six months	Oct £000	Nov £000	Dec £000	Jan £000	Feb £000	Mar £000
Fixed assets	230	229	227	226	224	223
Current assets						
Debtors	224	223	245	265	255	305
Stock	317	455	559	580	507	406
	541	678	804	845	762	7
Current liabilities						
Creditors (inc VAT etc)	285	383	440	472	334	255
Hire purchase	20	20	19	19	18	18
Bank	143	181	239	252	268	253
Directors' loans	15	15	15	15	15	15
Tax	15	15	15	-	-	-
	478	614	728	758	635	541
Net current assets	63	64	76	87	127	170
	293	293	303	313	351	393
Mortgage loan	18	18	18	18	18	18
Deferred tax	41	41	41	41	41	41
	234	234	244	254	292	334
Share capital						
Revenue reserves	233	233	243	253	291	333
	234	234	244	254	292	334
Expected letter of credit requirement	100	150	175	200	100	100

RATIOS AND OTHER INFORMATION

As at 31 March	Year A	Year B	Year C	30 September Year C
Liquidity				
Credit given (days)	53	48	52	38
Credit taken (days)	123	155	70	69
Stock turnover (days)	110	88	87	69
Current ratio	1.26:1	1.29:1	1.22:1	1.12:1
Acid test	0.48:1	0.53:1	0.51:1	0.44:1
Profitability				
Gross margin (%)	21.9	21.6	18.7	18.0
Net margin (%)	3.9	2.0	2.5	2.4
Financial structure				
Gearing (%) (Directors' loans as capital)	111	73	104	94
Interest cover (times)	4.5	2.5	3.0	2.7
Net working assets to sales (%)	27	18	23	26
Retained profit to sales (%)	3.4	1.3	1.6	2.4

concerned) are ignored, borrowing is increasing steadily and there is a significant hard core developing. The projections suggest that the worsening trend will continue.

The projections for the next six months look optimistic compared with past performance, indicating as they do a profit of £107,000, which is far in excess of what has been achieved in recent years and in the first six months of the year.

The directors' 'story' as to what can be achieved looks exceptionally demanding. So how safe would the bank be if things went wrong? There is a small equity in the value of the company's property but the main security for the bank has to be the current assets. At the proposed peak exposure next January, the cover indicated will be:

	£
Debtors	265,000
Stock	580,000
	845,000

This security has to cover:

	£
Overdraft	252,000
Documentary credits	200,000
	452,000

Documentary credits have to be included in the security cover calculation because, in the event of the company's running into liquidity problems, they will turn into borrowing as the bank has to meet the obligation it has given to the creditors. The underlying goods being supplied under the terms of the credits may add to the bank's security, but they should already be included in the projected stock figures.

So there is 187% cover by current assets for all liabilities and 59% cover by debtors. This cannot be enough to make the bank's position safe. The stock represents fashion garments, which will have a negligible break-up value, and even though the debtors are ostensibly good names, in all receiverships there are refusals to pay because of disputes over quality and so on, and a 75% realization proportion would probably be a realistic figure. On this basis, an overall realization of £200,000 might be expected to cover liabilities of £452,000.

A prudent lender would be very foolish therefore to provide additional facilities to Fatties Ltd. Their request involves a high level of risk, which cannot be covered by security. The business needs an injection of outside capital if it is going to expand at the rate considered desirable by its management.

Case 3

Mining Equipment Ltd currently banks with one of your competitors and has been a longstanding marketing target for your branch. The company was founded over 30 years ago and has been with its present bankers for most of that time. It manufactures, in a factory in a development area in the north of England, machinery used in the mining industry. By far its largest customer is British Coal.

Following a year-long strike in the British coal-mining industry, which ended in Year A, British Coal has been closing coal mines. Your Economics Department considers that this trend is likely to continue in the UK, although overseas mining markets may be more buoyant.

Mining Equipment Ltd has not found trading conditions easy since the end of the mining strike, and last year the directors decided to stop producing certain loss-making products. This involved closing down a department of the factory and making a number of employees redundant. After taking these steps the directors are confident that the business will have a healthy future.

The company currently enjoys an overdraft limit of £400,000, together with a medium-term loan of which the present balance is £255,000 with seven years of its term to run. These facilities are secured by a mortgage over the company's freehold and leasehold properties.

The directors have recently had their annual review meeting with their present bank, at which they produced their latest audited accounts, projections for the current financial year (see below), and management accounts for the first quarter of the current financial year. These management accounts show sales on target but also reveal a loss of £25,000, which the directors put down to temporary production difficulties following on from the rationalization at the factory. They still expect to be able to meet their profit target for the full year despite this setback.

Their bank has agreed to renew the limits, but is insisting on having additional security in the form of a debenture and personal guarantees from the directors. The directors consider that their present bank's stance is unreasonable, and approach you to take over the company's account without the benefit of the additional security.

This is a company that has been around for a long time and must have been profitable in the past. It has been badly hit by an event outside its control – the miners' strike. Its future market position looks difficult and, given its dependence on British Coal, things do not look likely to get any easier as further coal mine closures take place. The best market available for the company's profits is overseas. However, export sales have actually been declining, and there is no evidence that the directors intend to redirect their efforts. This must raise a question mark against the management.

MINING EQUIPMENT LTD
BALANCE SHEETS

	Year A £		Year B £		Year C £	
Current assets						
Cash	300		200	900		
Debtors	411,100		464,700	361,900		
Stock	539,100	950,500	609,300	1,074,200	548,800	911,600
Current liabilities						
Creditors	354,400		419,100		308,200	
Bank	147,000		164,900		280,800	
Current taxation	27,100		18,900		23,000	
Dividends	22,900	551,400	24,800	627,700	13,400	625,400
Net current assets		399,100		446,500		286,200
Fixed assets						
Freehold and leasehold deeds	194,700		187,000		171,300	
Plant and machinery	374,400	569,100	387,500	574,500	355,200	526,500
Total assets less current liabilities		968,200		1,021,000		812,700
Term and other liabilities						
Medium-term loans	275,200		293,500		267,000	
Deferred taxation	20,000	295,200	19,200	312,700	6,600	273,600
Net assets		673,000		708,300		539,100
Financed by						
Shared capital		300,000		300,000		300,000
Profit and loss account		373,000		408,300		239,100
Shareholders' funds		673,000		708,300		539,100

PROFIT AND LOSS ACCOUNT FIGURES

	Year A	Year B	Year C	Forecast: Year D
	£	£	£	£
Sales	1,584,100	2,069,800	1.932,900	1,987,100
inc. exports	487,000	446,100	391,200	362,000
Cost of sales	1,156,400	1,345,400	1,333,700	1,232,000
inc. purchases	631,000	696,800	591,300	601,200
Gross profit	427,700	724,400	599,200	755,100
Interest	46,700	50,600	47,700	62,600
Profits before tax and extraordinary items	(67,000)	142,000	73,400	164,800
Extraordinary items (restructuring and redundancy costs)	–	–	187,400	–

RATIOS AND OTHER INFORMATION

	Year A	Year B	Year C	Forecast: Year D
Net gearing	63%	65%	101%	
Interest cover (times)	–	3.8	2.5	
Credit given (days)	95	82	68	
Credit taken (days)	205	220	190	
Stock turnover (days)	170	165	150	
Current ratio	1.72:1	1.71:1	1.46:1	
Acid test	0.75:1	0.74:1	0.58:1	
Gross profit margin (%)	27	35	31	38
Net profit margin (%)	(4)	7	4	8

FUNDS FLOW FORECAST

Year D	Ist Qtr £	2nd Qtr £	3rd Qtr £	4th Qtr £	Year £
Profit before tax	8,800	45,400	47,100	63,500	164,800
Depreciation	22,200	22,200	24,700	24,600	93,700
Other items not involving movement of funds	600	600	600	700	2,500
Sales of fixed assets	900	900	900	800	3,500
	32,500	69,100	73,300	89,600	264,500
Capital expenditure	(57,200)	(1,200)	(52,500)	(52,500)	(163,400)
Tax paid	(6,400)	—	(23,000)	—	(29,400)
Dividends paid	—	(17,200)	—	(17,200)	(34,400)
Changes in working capital	38,800	(15,300)	10,500	(37,200)	(3,200)
(Increase)/decrease in net borrowing	7,700	35,400	8,300	(17,300)	34,100
From	(546,900)	(539,200)	(503,800)	(495,500)	(546,900)
To	(539 200)	(503,800)	(495,500)	(512,800)	(512,800)

The directors may be optimistic about the future, but this optimism is not supported by any hard evidence. Gearing has increased and interest cover declined, with both figures at an uncomfortable level for a manufacturing business making machinery of this type. If the directors have not now got things right and trading losses and/or further exceptional write-offs are made, these figures will get even worse. There is already evidence that things are not going well in the management accounts for the first quarter of the current year, where a profit of £8,800 was anticipated but a loss of £25,000 occurred. No matter what the excuses, this is disturbing.

Overall, sales and profitability have had no steady pattern over recent years. Given the recent difficult history of its major market this may not be surprising, but what inferences can be drawn from the figures seen? Year A was bound to be a bad year with the strike, but equally Year B was probably an unusually good year as British Coal would be re-equipping after the losses in the strike. The figures for Year C are probably the best guide for the future. This year showed a further considerable loss after extraordinary items, and questions have to be asked as to just how 'extraordinary' some of these were.

Future market conditions do not look at all rosy, but there is no suggestion anywhere that the directors are seeking to diversify. Such an exercise would undoubtedly be expensive in the short term, but it ought to be considered. Again, failure to look realistically at the future must raise a question mark against the management.

Liquidity is declining. Less credit is being given as the company tries to keep its borrowing down. Given that there is a dominant customer, this is a surprising trend, so how is it being achieved? It may be good management, but it would not be surprising to find that exceptional discounts are being given to encourage early payment. On the other side of the balance sheet, the company is able to obtain substantial credit from its suppliers, but this would not continue if there were any doubts about the company's future. In this context, the granting of a debenture by the company could have an adverse effect on the creditors, and any cut-back in credit would have to involve a higher borrowing requirement, which may not be sustainable.

The restructuring programme has had a beneficial effect on stock turnover. It does appear that manufacturing efficiency has improved, as represented by the lower level of stocks being carried.

The company's projections show a significant increase in both the gross and net profit margins over what has been achieved recently. It may be that further improvements in efficiency after the rationalization are possible, but the targets look very demanding, given the market conditions, and have not been achieved in the first quarter. Additionally, the funds flow forecast suggests that capital expenditure will run significantly ahead of the depreciation charge with the consequent further drain on cash resources.

The future of the company's business must be uncertain, so how safe would a lender's position be? The request for facilities without a debenture is totally unrealistic. The security provided by the deeds is of limited value, as its major property, the factory, is in a development area. In such locations there is often a surplus of modern factory space available, so the factory would probably prove difficult to sell and could easily not achieve book value.

Even with a debenture the bank's security position would be stretched. The book figures, as at the end of Year C, indicate the following position:

	£
Freehold and leasehold deeds	171,300
Debtors	361,900
Stock	548,000
	1,082,000

To cover:	
Overdraft	280,800
Medium-term loans	267,000
	547,800

Assuming the deeds realize 70% of book value, debtors 80% (they should be good: most of them are due from British Coal) and stock 25%, the following realizations would be seen:

	£
Deeds @ 70%	20,000
Debtors @ 80%	290,000
Stock @ 20%	137,000
	547,000

The debenture cover is at the barest minimum, and the borrowing figure does not take account of the fact that some of the increased facility will be used to reduce creditors rather than increase assets. If good profits are not earned – and it must be questionable that they will be – then the debenture cover will gradually decrease. Directors' guarantees, provided these are worth something, would be essential if the bank is going to give the management the opportunity to prove that their recovery plan can work. Whatever happens, the company's bankers are probably in for a bumpy ride over the next few months, and it is not an account that a sensible banker would want to take over.

The actual business on which this case is based was unable to find alternative bankers, and after trading on for a few months was sold to a company that was better able to make use of the company's strengths, particularly its good product range, and provide the necessary capital for diversification.

Case 4

Spinster Wools Ltd manufacture hand-knitting wool yarns mainly sold direct to retailers. They have banked with you for over 30 years and until recently have always been profitable, despite periods when hand-knitting has gone out of fashion.

Two years ago there was a sudden drop in the market for hand-knitting wools. The directors of Spinster expected this drop to be temporary, but market conditions have continued to worsen. A recent article in the *Financial Times* has speculated that the market for hand-knitting wools might reduce by a further 20% before any recovery takes place.

The company currently has an overdraft limit of £500,000. Last year, as a condition of continuing the facility, you took a debenture as security with a formula of 1½ times cover of the overdraft by debtors and 2½ times by debtors and stock. Recently there has been pressure on the limit, excesses have occurred, and the debenture formula has been breached.

SPINSTER WOOLS LTD
BALANCE SHEET

As at 31 December	Year A £	Year A £	Year B £	Year B £	Year C £	Year C £	Draft Year D £	Draft Year D £
Current assets								
Cash	2,122		2,139		1,933		1,290	
Debtors	648,374		669,281		591,695		588,071	
Stock	852,919	1,503,415	766,446	1,437,866	846,077	1,439,705	818,302	1,407,663
Current liabilities								
Creditors	498,993		492,958		457,516		572,078	
Bank overdraft	329,541		277,820		440,027		498,847	
Current tax	90,915		29,895		54,737			
Future tax	68,083	987,532	89,080	883,753	56,821	1,009,101	–	1,070,925
Net current assets		515,883		548,113		430,604		336,738
Fixed assets								
Leasehold improvements	54,334		80,944		102,561		98,732	
Plant and machinery	301,800	356,134	381,674	462,618	390,713	493,274	342,710	441,442
Net assets		872,017		1,010,731		923,878		778,180
Financed by:								
Issued share capital		150,000		150,000		150,000		150,000
Profit and loss account		722,017		860,731		773,878		628,180
		872,017		1,010,731		923,878		778,180

SPINSTER WOOLS LTD *continued*

PROFIT AND LOSS ACCOUNT SUMMARY

12 months to 31 December	Year A £	Year B £	Year C £	Draft Year D £
Sales	2,607,632	2,812,816	2,249,371	2,122,381
Gross profit	288,546	413,030	142,748	97,633
Net profit (loss) before tax	143,028	250,393	(79,464)	(145,698)

RATIOS AND OTHER INFORMATION

	Year A	Year B	Year C	Draft Year D
Current ratio	1.52:1	1.62:1	1.43:1	1.31:1
Acid test	0.66:1	0.75:1	0.59:1	0.55:1
Credit given (days)	91	87	96	101
Credit taken (days)	170	169	192	222
Stock turnover (days)	134	117	147	148
Gross margin (%)	11.1	14.7	6.3	4.6
Net margin (%)	5.5	8.9	(3.5)	(6.9)
Net gearing (%)	36	27	47	64
Interest cover (times)	3.8	4.3	–	–

DEBENTURE FIGURES (CURRENT YEAR TO DATE)

	Jan. £000	Feb. £000	Mar. £000	Apr. £000
Debtors	623	614	595	582
Stock	798	805	821	840
	1,421	1,419	1,416	1,422
Bank overdraft	470	511	505	499
Creditors	621	601	616	642
Liquid surplus	330	307	295	281
Net capital expenditure since last report	–	2	–	–

The directors have sent you a copy of draft accounts for last year (Year D). They now call and tell you:

(a) they require an increased overdraft limit of £600,000 to see the company over the traditionally poor summer sales period;

(b) their auditors are of the opinion that they should write down the value of stocks by £300,000;

(c) they will be unable to restore the debtor element of the debenture formula and, if the stock write-down takes place, will not be able to meet the stock and debtor element. They wish the formula to be reduced to 1 times debtors and 2 times debtors and stock.

The situation described here is not unusual if a company is undertrading. The directors' request is essentially to replace capital the company has lost through its poor trading by bank borrowing. As it has lost capital that previously supported assets, it is also having to ask the bank to accept a reduced level of security cover. Not a happy situation.

Like Mining Equipment Ltd, Spinster Wools Ltd has obviously been a successful business in the past, and the profit performance in Years A and B was good, with borrowing and interest cover at acceptable levels. However, it is a one-product company trapped in a declining market where conditions are unlikely to improve in the immediate future. There is no indication that the management are doing anything significant to put the matter right. Where is the rationalization programme, redundancies and so on? While such action is unpleasant to take, it is necessary if the company is going to slim down to a level justified by the nature of the market.

Capital expenditure in the recent past has been funded by short-term borrowing, and while gearing is at acceptable levels, it is deteriorating. Given that the stocks appear to be overvalued by £300,000, the true figure for net tangible assets would also be £300,000 lower at, say, £478,000. This puts the true gearing figure at over 100% and indicates that the losses (and/or profits in earlier years) have not reflected the true (poorer) level of trading performance.

The business is becoming increasingly illiquid. The current ratio and acid test look just about acceptable in the recent accounts but again have been favourably distorted by the false stock figure. The debenture figures since the end of the last financial year show a continuing deterioration in the liquid surplus, and after the £300,000 stock write-off there will in fact be a liquid deficit.

Given the cash flow pressures, it is surprising to see the rising trend in credit given. Hand-knitting wools are very often sold through small specialist retailers, who must also be having a hard time in the poorer market. Are all the debtors going to be good? Probably not. The poor stock turnover ratio reflects the unsaleable stocks identified by the auditors, and credit taken is rising to uncomfortable levels. There must be some creditor pressure on the business now, and it is not surprising that a higher overdraft limit is needed.

Profitability has been declining steadily as sales fall and margins are squeezed. The debenture figures indicate further losses. The reduction in liquid surplus in the absence of a significant element of capital expenditure gives a good idea of the extent of the trading losses since December. This is despite the fact that the winter is the company's 'good' trading period. With the predicted further market fall and the advent of the poorer summer season, things are going to get worse rather than better.

The pressure on the overdraft limit is not surprising, nor are the excesses. The debenture figures show a hard core in the overdraft, which cannot be far short of the limit. The business undoubtedly needs an urgent cash injection to keep it afloat.

If the bank increased the limit, would it be safe? An analysis of the security position is needed. Stock will have only limited value in a break-up, and it is to the debtors that the bank will have to look. The present 1½ times cover formula is probably as low as a bank would want to go. Once cover is not going to be enough, and although twice cover by current assets looks comforting, the stock will only have significant value if the business can be sold as a going concern.

The bank ought to have reacted sooner to the company's failure to maintain the debenture formula. Relaxing a debenture formula is exactly the same thing as releasing security and so should be done only when the bank's risk has reduced because, say, other security has been made available. This is not the case here, and the directors are asking the bank to assume more risk with less security. A reasonable assessment of the bank's security position, based on the April debenture figures, will be:

	£000
Debtors – say 60% April figure	349
Stock – say 25% April figure (reduced by £300,000 stock write-off)	135
	484
To cover borrowing	499

With some realizations from the leasehold premises and plant and machinery, the bank is probably only just covered now. If losses continue, as seems likely, and borrowing is allowed to increase to £600,000, a significant proportion of which will be used to reduce creditors, there will be a significant security shortfall. In fact, more security, perhaps in the form of supported directors' guarantees, is probably necessary simply to continue the present £500,000 overdraft limit.

The spectre of receivership looms for Spinster Wools Ltd. However, banks simply do not put longstanding customers into receivership without an attempt to save them. There is in fact a shortage of good management information on which to base any decision. Would it be possible to make the business viable by taking some of the remedial action set out in Chapter 9 of *Bankers' Lending Techniques?* A thorough investigation of the company is required, and this will have to be done by someone independent of the directors. The bank's most likely course of action will therefore be to appoint investigating accountants to report on the viability of the business and the way forward.

4

Capital expenditure proposals

Definition of capital expenditure

It is relatively easy to identify items that everyone would think of as being capital expenditure. The two most obvious are investment in a new or larger set of premises, and the purchase of extra plant and machinery. Other items can also be regarded as capital expenditure for example, the purchase of another business.

In the previous chapter, I defined working capital as 'oiling the wheels' of a business. Capital expenditure investment clearly does more than this. It is essentially one-off, and is not absolutely necessary for the immediate day-to-day working of a business. It is often large, and aimed at bringing about large future changes in the way a business operates. It ought to bring about a longer-term improvement in the performance of the business, and because this improved performance will be spread over a number of future years, it may be appropriate to finance the expenditure over a term.

Capital investment appraisal

The fundamental objective of any investment ought to be that in return for paying out a given amount of cash today, a larger amount will be received back over a period of time. Therefore a logical approach to a company's capital investment decisions requires that quite complex calculations are carried out to ensure that the expenditure will be worthwhile. Despite this, it is clear that many companies are not particularly rational, and embark on significant investment projects purely because the management consider them to be 'a good idea'.

The first thing a lender needs to do is be satisfied that the customer has undertaken a realistic and structured assessment of the implications. There are four main ways of assessing capital expenditure projects:

(a) *Pay-back* – This method calculates the time taken to recoup the initial outlay.

(b) *Return on Investment* – This method calculates the average annual return as a percentage of either the average or the total amount of the investment.

(c) *Net Present Value Return on Investment* – This method discounts the future revenues from the project to show the return adjusted for the time value of money (cash received now is more valuable than cash received in the future because it can be invested to earn an income in the intervening period).

(d) *Yield (or Internal Rate of Return)* – This method uses the same principles as a Net Present Value approach, but with the objective of establishing the discount rate at which the present values of the cash inflows and outflows match.

It is generally accepted that the methods that involve discounting cash flows – that is, methods 3 and 4 above – give the most accurate assessment of the return from an investment project. However, it also needs to be recognized that discounted cash flow techniques are complex and difficult for many non-accountant businessmen to understand. This is not the place for a detailed analysis of the advantages and disadvantages of discounting cash flows, and the subject is very well covered in Chapter 11 of *Accountancy for Banking Students* by Edwards and Mellett (3rd edn, 1991).

What is worth emphasizing is the importance of a business's performance in the initial periods after the investment is made. Because, over time, the net present value of money declines, costs and income in the immediate future have a proportionately higher impact on the viability of a project. So, in simple terms, to be viable a capital investment project usually needs to be generating a positive return in its early stages. A commonsense approach is to concentrate on the next one or two years' performance, to determine whether the investment can be financed. If it can, the remaining periods can probably be left to look after themselves.

Sustainable cash flow

Predicting working capital needs usually involves forecasting over a period of not more than 12 months. The short-term lender is able to look to known, or relatively easily ascertainable, cash flows. However, in assessing capital expenditure proposals, the risks are likely to be medium-term, and more emphasis has to be put on the underlying strengths and weaknesses of the business. The key elements will be the quality and range of the company's products and markets, the quality and depth of management, the economic outlook for the industry, the company's forward strategy, and the financial implications that arise from these elements.

The company will have to have the capacity to produce sustainable cash flow surpluses to repay borrowing over a term. As always, forecasts need to be tested against past performance, as a lender is much more likely to feel comfortable if a customer has demonstrated the capacity to generate regular cash surpluses in the past. An examination of the company's recent sources and application of funds statements will provide the best guide to the business's historic cash-generating capacity.

Unfortunately, sources and application of funds statements are not, at present, always presented in the most 'user friendly' form. The accountancy bodies are currently addressing general criticisms about the way statements are set out, but most lenders have extraction forms that logically identify the various cash inflows and outflows during the year, with the net funding requirement/surplus being the bottom line.

A cash requirement overall is not in itself a bad sign – it may represent one year's heavy capital expenditure programme – and it is the trend over a period of years that is important. A continuous pattern of substantial cash shortages would tend to suggest that a business would not be able to generate funds to repay a medium-term borrowing.

Analysis needs to focus on the most significant reasons for a surplus or deficit. Again, concentration needs to be not on one particular year, but on the overall performance over a number of years. The three main areas will usually be:

(a)   working capital variation;

(b)   operating cash flow;

(c)   capital expenditure/depreciation.

Working capital variation
In periods of inflation, most companies need to increase working capital, even on a

APPLIED LENDING TECHNIQUES

static level of sales. Capital expenditure projects involving expansion of fixed assets will usually have an underlying aim of increasing sales, often substantially. What impact will this have on the working capital requirement? An analysis of the historic working capital variation in comparison with past sales growth will enable a view to be taken as to whether sales can be expanded quickly without a major working capital finance requirement.

Operating cash flow

This line in the sources and application of funds statement will demonstrate the extent to which the company is generating sufficient funds to cover its operations, service its debts and meet its tax obligations, before any other external payments or application of funds to maintain or expand its fixed assets. If it is not sufficiently positive, there needs to be a degree of healthy scepticism about whether the business's future plans can produce the extra cash flow needed to cover future repayments.

Capital expenditure/depreciation

A major capital expenditure project may obviate the need for capital expenditure in the immediate future. However, it is unlikely that all capital expenditure will stop, and if, for example, the project is to enlarge a factory, there will be a continuing need to replace machinery and equipment, and so on. Generally speaking, new and improved machinery costs more than the equipment it replaces, so typically the capital expenditure charge can be expected to run ahead of the amount being set aside for depreciation. It will be the extent of the difference between the regular capital expenditure charge and depreciation that will be of interest, as this will demonstrate the amount that has to be funded each year before cash is available to meet repayments on a loan.

Case 1
....

Soft and Hard Ltd was formed nine years ago by two young computer experts. It operates from premises in the south-east of England, about 50 miles from London. The company adapts and supplies computer hardware for specific purposes, designs computer software, and provides technical support for companies with computer systems. It has banked with you since its formation and has an overdraft limit of £300,000 secured by a standard form of debenture. It has over 1,000 customers, including a number of large public companies, and you are aware that it is often able to obtain advance payments on individual contracts.

Although Soft and Hard Ltd made losses during its early years, it has recently been performing well and has outgrown its present rented premises. The company has the opportunity to acquire a site nearby with planning permission for 17,500 square feet of offices. It would initially require only 12,500 square feet, and the rest would be let to bring in £40,000 per annum in rent. Local authority rates at £3 per square foot, and other expenses on the leased portion, would be borne by the tenants.

The cost of the site is £300,000, and the building is estimated to cost a further £1.3 million to erect and fit out. Over the past 12 months the company's bank account has operated in credit, and it currently has a credit balance of £300,000 available to put towards the project.

The directors have not yet started preparing their budgets for Year E, but they see no reason why sales and profits should not continue to grow at their present rates.

They are aware that other parties are interested in acquiring the site, which is uniquely convenient both for their existing workforce and for contact with suppliers. They wish to exchange contracts immediately, and ask you to provide a 20-year medium-term loan of £1.3 million in addition to continuing the current overdraft limit.

The company is a longstanding customer with a good track record over recent years, and its bank would want to help fund its expansion, if at all possible. The main problem with the request is that at first glance the new premises look ambitiously large, and it is never a good thing to be put under time pressure to agree a medium-term facility without proper information. Some cool analysis is needed.

The amount requested at £1.3 million does not seem to include legal costs, and, while fitting-out costs are said to be included, whether this includes furnishing and so on is not clear. In fact the whole nature of the building estimates is somewhat vague – have the directors got firm quotations from builders, and will the building contract be at a fixed price? Who is to do the building, and will the construction company be acceptable to the bank? If satisfactory answers to these questions cannot be obtained, there could well be cost overruns, which would involve a higher-finance requirement than that requested.

The historical accounts show a good recent performance by the business. The previous high levels of gearing have been eliminated. The sources and application of funds statement shows a strong operating cash flow. Despite the rapid expansion of sales,

SOFT AND HARD LIMITED
BALANCE SHEETS

As at 31 December	Year A £	£	Year B £	£	Year C £	£
Current assets						
Cash	1,200		1,400		46,134	
Debtors	612,008		771,338		1,212,066	
Stock	263,473	876,681	503,696	1,276,434	669,674	1,927,874
Current liabilities						
Creditors	680,117		1,014,284		1,543,398	
Hire purchase	61,652		116,526		182,063	
Bank	128,348		107,338			
Current tax	17,000	887,117	42,500	1,280,648	109,336	1,834,797
Net current assets		(10,436)		(4,214)		93,077
Fixed assets						
Plant and machinery		183,800		222,745		296,746
Net assets		£173,364		£218,531		389,823
Financed by:						
Ordinary shares		100,000		100,000		100,000
Profit and loss account		73,364		118,531		289,823
		173,364		218,531		389,823

PROFIT AND LOSS ACCOUNT SUMMARY

12 months to 31 December	Year A £	Year B £	Year C £
Sales	2,573,227	3,002,325	4,809,524
Gross profit	1,340,142	1,402,041	2,262,282
Net profit before tax	54,567	73,667	280,883

SOFT AND HARD LIMITED *continued*
SOURCES AND APPLICATIONS OF FUNDS

	Year A £	Year B £	Year C £
Profit before tax	54,567	73,667	280,883
Depreciation	97,644	114,667	144,231
Adjustment for other items not involving the movement of funds	(7,644)	(7,765)	(11,202)
Tax paid	–	(3,000)	(42,755)
Working capital variation	(48,669)	(13,991)	(9,871)
Operating cash now	95,898	163,578	361,286
Disposal of fixed assets	33,459	19,708	15,315
Capital expenditure	(89,102)	(162,076)	(224,529)
Cash available for investment	40,255	21,210	152,072
Decrease in short-term debt			
Increase in cash balances	40,255	21,210	152,072

RATIOS AND OTHER INFORMATION

	Year A	Year B	Year C
Net gearing (%)	109	102	
Interest cover (times)	2.0	2.4	7.8
Credit given (days)	85	84	75
Credit taken (days)	242	221	183
Stock turnover (days)	98	100	84
Current ratio	0.99:1		1.05
Acid test	0.69:1	0.60:1	0.69:1
Gross profit margin (%)	52	47	47
Net profit margin (%)	2.1	2.5	5.8

MANAGEMENT ACCOUNTS

	Actual 6 months to 30 June Year D		Budget 6 months to 31 December Year D	
	£	£	£	£
Sales		3,029,250 (100%)		3,068,900 (100%)
Cost of sales		(1,600,916)		(1,534,450)
Gross profit		1,428,334 (47%)		1,534,450 (50%)
Overheads including:		(1,232,180)		(1,290,350)
rent and rates	30,617		33,400	
depreciation	86,187		103,500	
finance charges	12,838		18,300	
Profit before tax		196,154 (6.5%)		244,100 (8.0%)

very little extra working capital has been needed. The reason for this must be because the company is able to obtain advance payments on a large proportion of its sales. Provided this can continue, expansion on the working capital front can largely be self-funded. However, it needs to be recognized that problems could arise should the big customers not be prepared to meet the company's advance payment terms in future.

The company's strong cash position will disappear once the loan has been drawn, and gearing will initially go over 200%, with interest cover weakening commensurately. However, profitability is good and the gross margin has been very stable, given the rapid expansion. The company's historic track record is that it has been able to expand turnover without reducing profit margins, which gives a lot of comfort that it will be able to do this in the future.

The company cannot get away without producing some formal projections showing how repayment is to be achieved. However, we know enough about the business to reach some informed conclusions without them. As stated above, little extra working capital will be needed but capital expenditure is running ahead of depreciation and is likely to continue to do so – this is a high tech business – so not all net profit will be available to meet repayments. Repayments on £1.3 million over, say, 20 years (at, say, 13%) would be £181,000 per annum. £40,000 of this figure can be met from subletting (provided it can be established that tenants are readily available). The extra costs of the new building (for example, rates will be £37,500 on the unleased portion) can be offset by the saving in rent and rates on the old property of £64,000. Given the profit performance seen in the management accounts to date, overall it will be surprising if in the new building profits were not over £500,000 next year.

The security position should be sound. A new standard office block in the south-east of England should produce a valuation at around cost, and this would give approximately 123% cover for the loan. A professional valuation will be needed. This security margin might be considered to be a little thin, but there will be surplus security cover in the form of the debenture over the current assets, which will of course also have to cover the overdraft facility. There is a potential problem with the company's debtors, in that they represent contract monies, which can sometimes break up badly. However, the debtors appear to be well spread, and this should provide some comfort. Keyman cover over the directors will be essential, given their importance to the business.

On the information given, despite all the favourable indications, formal approval to the loan cannot be agreed without reservation. However, a positive indication will be necessary in the circumstances and an agreement in principle can be given, in view of the width of the margin between the likely level of repayments and expected profitability. Final agreement would be conditional on:

(a) sight of building cost estimates and so on, and a professional valuation of the building, including its value when completed;

(b) projections for the new business, assuming a move to the new building, although these will have to be very dismal indeed for the loan not to be viable.

Case 2

....

Copycat Ltd duplicate video cassettes of films and so on, on behalf of distributors for sale or rent in the UK. The UK duplicating market currently stands at £150 million and is growing at the rate of 25% per annum. The company was established five years ago by two brothers, Sidney and George Walsh, who are in their mid-40s. It has banked with you since its formation.

Their duplicating process uses standard video cassette recorders, each recording a new cassette in 'real time'. They have over 750 machines producing on average 10 cassettes each per day. A new type of duplicating machine is now available that will copy 120 tapes per hour against one copy per hour by a standard 'real time' recorder. The new machines will also produce better-quality pictures and will be cheaper to maintain. The directors wish to purchase a number of these new machines at a total cost of £500,000. These machines will cope with the company's immediate expansion needs.

The directors have a strong relationship with a finance company, which has provided medium-term loans to fund past capital expenditure. These loans are secured on the machinery plus directors' guarantees supported by the equity in their houses worth £350,000.

The bank provides an overdraft limit of £125,000, which has occasionally been increased to meet seasonal peaks. This is secured by a debenture and unsupported directors' guarantees.

In the past there have been numerous excesses above the overdraft limit but no cheques have been returned. You have been reluctant to increase the limit because management information coming from the company has been spasmodic and you wished to maintain tight control.

The directors call to see you, bringing with them their new finance director, who is an experienced accountant. They tell you that the finance director has been given a brief to improve their management information and controls. They wish to borrow £500,000 over five years to buy the new machines, and they believe the bank would be a cheaper source of funds than the finance company.

This business is operating in a rapidly growing market, which is likely to continue to expand. The financial information suggests that the company had some difficulty in its earlier years (nil net tangible assets in Year A), which its management have brought it through.

The company has ambitious expansion plans, and is seeking to increase market share (sales projected to rise 63% against the market 25%). Moreover, production technology is changing. There must be a risk that the company will end up as a high-cost producer if its competitors are able to adapt more quickly. A continuing high level of capital expenditure is likely to be required because the company will need to replace its existing duplicating machines and may also have to spend money on premises and so on, to cope with the expansion.

There is evidence of poor control over finances. There have been excesses over the overdraft limit, and it would not be surprising if there had been creditor pressure. Credit taken has increased and credit given reduced, indicating cash flow problems. However, given the size of the debtor book, with the benefit of better financial information the bank might well have been prepared to increase the overdraft to help fund the increased turnover. Certainly, coping with sales in excess of £2.5 million on a £125,000 overdraft limit calls for a lot of juggling with the sources of working capital. The appointment of the new accountant will be a very positive feature if he can bring more professionalism to bear.

As might be expected, capital expenditure is running significantly ahead of the depreciation charge, and may well continue to do so. However, operating cash flow in Year C is strongly positive, and if the sales and profits targets in the projections can be achieved, there will be a strong performance in Year D. The projected sources and application of funds statement suggests that the expansion can be achieved without any additional working capital. This was possible in Year C, against the background of a substantial sales increase, so there is a form of track record.

As always, everything will depend on whether the projections can be achieved. The market ought to be good for a low-cost producer, and the anticipated improvement in gross profit margin ought to be possible, given the increased efficiency from the new machines. The proposed net profit margin is not very different from that already achieved and ought to be possible, even with the higher interest costs involved.

Usually, machinery is not worth taking as security, but the new equipment will be 'state of the art' and should keep its value well, at least in the immediate future. It will,

COPYCAT LIMITED
BALANCE SHEETS

As at 31 March	Year A £000	£000	Year B £000	£000	Year C £000	£000
Current assets						
Cash	1		2		1	
Debtors	332		919		968	
Stock	70	403	129	1,050	144	1,113
Current liabilities						
Creditors	121		367		430	
Bank	65		221		123	
Tax	–	(186)	–	(588)	39	(592)
Net current assets		217		462		521
Fixed assets						
Leasehold buildings	12		12		11	
Plant, machinery and motor vehicles	189	201	254	266	511	522
		418		728		1,043
Term liabilities						
Medium-term loans		(418)		(463)		(689)
Net assets		–		265		354
Financed by:						
Share capital		1		1		100
Profit and loss account		(1)		264		254
		–		265		354

PROFIT AND LOSS SUMMARY

As at 31 March	Year A £000	Year B £000	Year C £000	Projected: Year D £000
Sales	818	1,891	2,526	4,125
Gross profit	189	445	450	1,049
Profit before tax	86	259	185	310

SOURCE AND APPLICATION OF FUNDS STATEMENT

As at 31 March	Year A £000	Year B £000	Year C £000	Projected: Year D £000
Profit before tax	86	259	185	310
Depreciation	49	66	125	188
Adjustment for other items not involving the movement of funds	(2)	134	–	–
Tax paid	–	–	–	(39)
Working capital variation	(50)	(410)	(1)	(–)
Operating cash flow	83	49	309	459
Disposal of fixed assets	6	1	–	–
Capital expenditure	(96)	(132)	(381)	(500)
Extraordinary items	–	(129)	(56)	
Cash available for investment	(7)	(211)	(128)	(41)
(Increase)/Decrease in long-term debt	(27)	(55)	(226)	(350)
(Increase)/Decrease in net short-term debt	20	(156)	98	309
	(7)	(211)	(128)	(41)

RATIOS AND OTHER INFORMATION

	Year A	Year B	Year C	Projected: Year D
Net gearing (%)	–	257	229	113
Interest cover (times)	4.6	7.6	3.8	2.0
Credit given (days)	148	177	140	120
Credit taken (days)	97	54	110	110
Stock turnover (days)	35	25	24	21
Current ratio	2.16:1	1.78:1	1.88:1	1.69:1
Acid test	1.78:1	1.57:1	1.64:1	1.54:1
Gross profit margin (%)	23.1	23.5	17.8	25.4
Net profit margin (%)	10.5	13.7	7.3	7.5

BANK ACCOUNT

	Year A £000	Year B £000	Year C to date £000	£000
Average balance	45 Dr	98 Dr	91 Dr	

	Worst balance	Best balance	Average balance	Limit marked
Year B				
April/May/June	181 Dr	12 Cr	65 Dr	125 Dr
July/August/Sept	151 Dr	21 Dr	99 Dr	125 Dr
Oct/Nov/Dec	167 Dr	32 Dr	126 Dr	175 Dr
Year C				
Jan/Feb/March	158 Dr	16 Cr	102 Dr	125 Dr
April	119 Dr	33 Cr	72 Dr	125 Dr

therefore, be valuable security, although a chattel mortgage will be needed to ensure a fixed charge. Moreover, debtor cover under the debenture is very strong – nearly eight times bank borrowing at the Year C balance sheet date. It ought to be possible to achieve 1.75 times debtor cover for borrowing of, say, £625,000, and this, together with the machines, should be sufficient security. As always with longer-term borrowing, Keyman cover over the principal directors will be appropriate.

It has to be admitted that this proposition is marginal, with ambitious sales targets, potential further capital expenditure and possibly more working capital needed. However, market conditions are good, the management is experienced, at least in the sales field, and there should be adequate security. Provided good monitoring information can now be made available, it is probably worth a go.

Case 3

As part of your branch marketing programme, you have arranged for local estate agents to inform you when new businesses move into your area. One of your contacts has let you know that an executive employment and consultancy agency called No. 1 Staff Ltd is seeking to acquire an old warehouse near your branch, where planning permission has just been given for conversion to offices.

You arrange to meet the Managing Director of the company, a Mr Ginger, when he is next in the area. Ginger tells you the following:

(a)   He is entirely happy with his present bank but would be willing for you to quote for a bridging loan of £1.25 million, which would cover the purchase price and cost of refurbishment of the warehouse.

(b)   He does not intend to put his present premises on the market until the refurbishment of the warehouse is complete.

(c)   The business was established six years ago and has recently been going through a period of rapid expansion. It now has 95 employees of its own, operating in three separate locations – these will all be brought together in the new building.

Ginger promises to let you have a copy of the company's latest audited accounts, together with some outline management accounts and budget information. He is not prepared to let you have more detailed information or engage in longer discussions unless your Head Office will give an agreement in principle on the information available. The accounts and the other documents have arrived.

Although this proposition is framed as a bridging loan request and is therefore apparently short-term, the following analysis will show that it has to be dealt with in the context of a medium-term facility.

This is a new business opportunity for the bank. Some caution is required because the customers are coming in 'off the street', but the company has been established for six years and has shown rapid expansion in recent times.

Although the level of net assets at over £700,000 is considerable, this is largely as the result of a property revaluation rather than trading. In fact, the profits from trading for the first five years of the business's existence must have been fairly disappointing. In the past two years gearing has reduced considerably, but this is wholly due to the revaluation of the property. Gearing remains high, but it is fair to say that a large portion of the debt is medium- to long-term, which may make it sustainable. Interest cover is adequate, but it is disappointing to see the reducing trend in the actual figures. Of course, having only two years' accounts is less than ideal for establishing trends, but it is often the case that this is all a bank gets.

The current ratio and acid test are low, suggesting that the business may be short of

NO. 1 STAFF LIMITED
BALANCE SHEET

As at 31 May	Year A £	£	Year B £	£
Current assets				
Cash	9,036		24, 180	
Debtors	656,578		1, 1 55,404	
Stock	12,173	677,787	20,411	99,995
Current liabilities				
Creditors	583,008		856,567	
Hire purchase (less than 12 months)	35,178		25,048	
Bank overdraft	181,178		425,157	
Current portion of long-term debt	5,850		14,100	
Current taxation	14,784	819,998	98,932	1,419,804
Net current assets		(142,211)		(219,809)
Fixed assets				
Freehold land and buildings	233,613		1,086,096	
Plant, machinery and motor vehicle	195,176	428,789	255,274	1,341,370
Term liabilities				
Hire purchase (over 12 months)	52,756		31,308	
Long-term loans (secured by property)	164,550	(217,306)	387,501	(418,809)
		69,272		702,752
Financed by:				
Share capital		100		100
Revaluation reserve		–		523,369
Distributable reserves		69,172		179,283
		69,272		702,752

PROFIT AND LOSS ACCOUNT SUMMARY

	Year A	Year B	Budgets 12 months to 31 May Year C	4 months to 30 Sept. Year B Forecast	Actual
	£	£	£	£	£
Sales	2,685,374	5,234,983	7,398,000	2,433,000	2,111,842
Profit before tax	34,549	198,829	466,000	235,000	119,136
After:					
Interest paid	10,097	65,193	111,700	37,266	45,304
Depreciation	38,429	45,267	54,000	16,800	16,800
Directors' remuneration	47,298	63,663	85,000	20,000	20,000

RATIOS AND OTHER INFORMATION

	Year A	Year B	Year C Budget	4 months Year B Budget	Actual
Net gearing (%)	621	122	–	–	–
Interest cover	4.4x	4.0x	5.2x	7.3x	3.6x
Current ratio	0.83:1	0.84:1	–	–	–
Acid test	0.81:1	0.83:1	–	–	–
Credit given (days)	89	81	–	–	–
Credit taken (days)	83	90	–	–	–
Gross margin (%)	28.0	32.9	36.0	35.7	34.3
Net margin (%)	1.3	3.8	6.3	9.7	5.6
Net working assets to sales (%)	3.2	6.1	–	–	–
Retained profit to sales (%)	1.1	2.1	–	–	–

liquidity. This is borne out by the reduction in credit given and the increase in credit taken. However, the net working assets to sales and retained profits to sales ratios are reasonably close, suggesting that it may just be possible to fund the working capital needs of expansion by internal cash generation.

The absence of a sources and application of funds statement makes it difficult to assess liquidity trends, and shows how useful this particular piece of information is in credit assessment.

Profit margins are improving but are very thin, and it would not take much of a setback to put the company into loss. There is a substantial gross margin, which, set against the small net margin, suggests a high level of fixed overheads. This might cause a problem in a downturn. The projected sales target is ambitious, but sales doubled last year, so it may be attainable. A staff agency is the kind of business that might still perform well in a general economic downturn, and this fact will be of some comfort.

As put, the proposition is an open-ended bridging loan. However, given the book value of the present properties and the size of the present mortgage, there is likely to be a substantial shortfall. The figures are:

		£
Cost of new property		1,250,000
Less sale of present properties		1,086,000
		164,000
Add present mortgage		387,500
		551,500
Add interest (worst case, say £1.25m @ 13% for 12 months)		162,500
		714,000

So the bridging loan could be contemplated only if the bank is prepared to take on a long-term mortgage of this sort of size at the end of the day.

Some extra working capital will be needed as a result of the sales expansion, but it ought to be possible to contain the overdraft within a limit of, say, £500,000. This £500,000 added to, say, £750,000 of long-term loans and HP would give total maximum borrowing of £1.25 million. At a 13% interest rate the interest charge would therefore be £162,500, and the business ought to be able to meet this from profits, given that the current interest charge is over £65,000. This interest charge is significantly higher than that suggested in the budget, and while it may be unduly pessimistic, budgets are often drafted too optimistically. The difficulty that remains, without having a sources and application of funds statement, is to determine how much cash it would be reasonable to expect the business to generate to meet repayments. From the information given, we do not know. However, the bank would be well secured, provided it also had second charges on the properties to be sold subject, of course, to professional valuations.

In practice, the bank would probably want to do all the company's facilities, which would mean taking over the existing long-term mortgage and overdraft. These, together with the bridging loan, would make total potential exposure around £2.15 million, which would be secured by deeds whose cost value would be £2,336,000.

This is too tight, and a debenture picking up the debtors, currently £1.1 million but which will increase with sales expansion, should give sufficient margin to make the facilities safe.

The overall conclusion has to be that there is insufficient information here to reach a definite decision, but there is enough positive knowledge to make the proposition worth taking to Head Office to get some sort of favourable indication, even if this falls short of the agreement in principle sought.

Case 4

Matthews Rubber Ltd is an old family firm that has been in business and has banked with your bank since 1936. It is currently run by two brothers, Patrick and John Matthews, both in their early 40s, each of whom owns 50% of the company.

The company manufactures rubber mats for use in cars. These are sold mainly through motor accessory retailers. Over recent years there has been some friction between the brothers over possible diversification into other products, with John wishing to change the business, and Patrick wanting to keep it much as it is now. John has now told Patrick that he wishes to go off on his own, and intends selling his shares. Patrick wishes to retain control of the company and asks you if you will assist him to do this by financing a 'buy-back' by the company of John's shares.

The brothers have recently had a professional valuation carried out of the company's freehold factory, which has revealed a hidden reserve of £290,000. After taking this into account, a price of £500,000 has been agreed for John's shares. £300,000 is to be paid immediately with the rest at £15,000 per annum. While money is owed to him, John will have a first charge over the factory. There will also be an annual interest charge in line with the previous year's inflation rate.

The company currently has a £300,000 overdraft facility, which you provide on an unsecured basis. Patrick Matthews asks you to continue this and also to provide a £300,000 medium-term loan over 10 years to cover the cost of the share buy-back. A one-year capital repayment holiday is requested.

As has been mentioned above, the purchase of a business financed by borrowed money is a capital expenditure proposition. Usually a business purchase will involve the acquisition of additional assets and profit-generating capacity, which will help to repay any long-term borrowing. However, in this instance the business is buying out one of its shareholders, so there will be no additional income to help meet borrowing costs, and in fact by substituting borrowing for a shareholder's capital the company's balance sheet will be weakened.

The company is a longstanding customer, and its bankers would wish to be positive, if at all possible. Moreover, as there has been a conflict between the two main directors over where the business is going in the future, there may well be problems in store for the company if no break is made.

The first thing to be established when looking at a business purchase is whether the price to be paid for the shares is reasonable. Purely on an asset basis, the draft net tangible assets, together with the hidden reserve in the property, give a value of around £1 million, so £500,000 for 50% looks fair.

However, companies are not valued solely on the net value of their assets, and some regard needs to be given to the profit-earning capacity of the business. In other words, the price being paid for the shares needs to be compared with the return that can be expected from the investment. The ratio that does this is the price/earnings ratio (P/E). The earnings figure is the after-tax profit of the business because it is the return to the investor that is at issue. The P/E ratio based on the last audited accounts calculated on a price of £500,000 looks very generous at 45 times. Using the draft figures, it comes down to 23 times but this, too, is very generous. An ordinary investor in this kind of business might well want a 20% return, which would suggest a P/E ratio of only 5 times. Patrick Matthews is not a totally disinterested investor, but the price he seems willing to pay seems to assume that the profit targets of at least the Year E projections will be met.

Is this likely? The projections look optimistic. The company's sales grew by 11% over the past two years, but are planned to grow by 43% over the next three years, including a near 10% rise in the current year. Why should this be possible? The gross and net margins are also predicted to rise steadily, and projections for credit given, credit taken and stock turnover all require improved performance.

In the past the business has not had to work under financial pressure. It has always

MATTHEWS RUBBER LTD
BALANCE SHEETS

As at 30 June	Year A		Year B		Draft Year C	
	£	£	£	£	£	£
Current assets						
Cash	200		100		100	
Debtors	359,200		361,800		620,000	
Stock	431,500	790,900	437,200	799,100	359,300	979,400
Current liabilities						
Creditors	289,600		336,400		395,300	
Bank	181,300		182,700		349,100	
Hire purchase	1,100		900		500	
Dividends	4,400		10,000			
Current tax	37,000	(513,400)	54,900	(584,900)		(744,900)
Net current assets		277,500		214,200		234,500
Term liabilities						
Deferred taxation	60,300		69,700		72,900	
Hire purchase	30,600	(90,900)	22,300	(92,000)	10,000	(82,900)
Fixed assets						
Freehold land and buildings	250,200		241,600		238,900	
Plant and machinery	264,900	515,100	345,000	586,600	314,100	553,000
Net assets		701,700		708,800		704,600
Financed by:						
Share capital		60,000		60,000		60,000
Profit and loss account		641,700		648,800		644,600
		701,700		708,800		704,600

PROJECTED BALANCE SHEETS

As at 30 June	Year D £	Year D £	Year E £	Year E £	Year F £	Year F £
Current assets						
Cash	100		100		100	
Debtors	680,900		737,700		791,400	
Stock	374,700	1,055,700	403,700	1,141,500	423,900	1,215,400
Current liabilities						
Creditors	425,800		505,600		590,000	
Bank	296,700		178,700		30,200	
Hire purchase	300		300		300	
		(722,800)		(684,600)		(620,500)
Net current assets		332,900		456,900		594,900
Term liabilities						
Deferred taxation	72,900		72,900		72,900	
Hire purchase	10,000		2,300			
Bank loan	300,000		300,000		267,800	
Deferred share purchase	200,000	(582,900)	185,000	(560,200)	170,000	(510,700)
		(250,000)		(103,300)		84,200
Fixed assets						
Freehold land and buildings	523,000		516,300		510,100	
Plant and machinery	299,100	822,100	264,300	780,600	232,900	743,000
Net assets		572,100		677,300		827,200
Financed by:						
Share capital		30,000		30,000		30,000
Capital reserve		290,000		290,000		290,000
Profit and loss account		252,100		357,300		507,200
		572,100		677,300		827,200

PROFIT & LOSS ACCOUNT SUMMARY

12 months to 30 June	Year A £	Year B £	Year C Draft £	Year D Projected £	Year E Projected £	Year F Projected £
Sales	1,887,700	2,042,300	2,096,000	2,300,000	2,630,000	3,000,000
Gross profit	530,700	558,300	565,900	630,800	743,500	860,900
Interest paid	27,200	25,100	28,300	86,500	70,500	50,000
Net profit before tax	59,600	57,900	79,000	105,800	174,200	243,000
After tax profit	28,300	22,300	43,500	65,500	113,200	157,900

RATIOS AND OTHER INFORMATION

	Year A	Year B	Year C	Year D	Year E	Year F
Net gearing (%)*	30	29	51	106	71	36
Interest cover (times)	3.2	3.3	3.8	2.2	3.5	5.9
Credit given (days)	69	65	108	108	102	96
Credit taken (days)	61	67	75	80	80	75
Stock turnover (days)	101	87	90	85	83	81
Current ratio	1:1.54	1:1.37	1:1.31	1:1.46	1:1.67	1:1.95
Acid test	0.72:1	0.62:1	0.83:1	0.94:1	1:1.07	1:1.28
Gross profit margin (%)	28.1	27.3	27.0	27.4	28.3	28.7
Net profit margin (%)	3.2	2.8	3.7	4.6	6.6	8.1

* Assumes deferred share purchase debt is not counted as borrowing.

been reasonably liquid, but this is about to change. Moreover, profitability has been less than impressive, with low net margins. Gearing is currently at a satisfactory level, and interest cover is also acceptable, but the business shows no recent record of being able to generate large amounts of cash.

The projected gearing figure should arguably include the deferred share purchase, which is in the form of a loan, so gearing in Year D would be 141% (rather than 106%). No significant capital expenditure is planned, although there has been none recently. This is a manufacturing business, and machinery will have to be replaced.

There is a need for sensitivity analysis to test whether the performance at or near present levels will be adequate to repay £500,000 over an acceptable term. However, the indications are that it would not.

Given the risks involved, any bank would want to have the facility well secured. The security available, assuming the debenture, would be:

	£		£
Freehold factory	523,000	@ 60%	314,000
less first mortgage	200,000		200,000
	323,000		114,000
Debtors say	600,000	@ 70%	420,000
Stock say	360,000	@ 25%	90,000
	960,000		510,000

A total of £624,000 worth of security to cover £600,000 of borrowing facilities – just enough. The security position could be strengthened by insisting that John Matthews's mortgage over the factory ranks after the bank.

He may refuse this, but in any event there is a strong case to be made for him ranking only *pari passu* with the bank.

This is a very marginal decision, and more information in the form of sensitivity analysis is required before a firm conclusion can be reached. The indications are that the plan is too ambitious, but some reconstruction of the proposition may be possible, perhaps involving an injection of capital from some outside investor.

Speculative builders

5

Introduction

A speculative builder is an individual or a company that carries out construction work without having definite sales arranged in advance. The typical case is a builder developing a housing estate. Any manufacturer relies on skill and judgement to produce goods that it is hoped the public will buy. A builder of houses is no different, but it is necessary to bear in mind that because a considerable cost is incurred in building a house, the risk to the builder – and the lender providing the finance – is that much greater. In Chapter 10 of *Bankers' Lending Techniques* I set out a theoretical framework for dealing with these additional risks.

However, while speculative builders have to be dealt with in a special manner, it is important to understand why. Many lenders have an obsession with simply applying preconceived formulae to building advances. Everyone knows about lending half the cost of land and two-thirds of the cost of development, or two-thirds of the cost of land and half the cost of development, or a combination of the two – two-thirds of both land and development costs. There is also a general willingness to allow building companies to borrow up to 200% of net tangible assets (200% gearing springs naturally from being prepared to lend on a one-third/two-thirds basis). These formulae are useful rules of thumb, but they are not tablets of stone.

They cannot be used in all circumstances, and an appreciation is needed of when they can be used and when they cannot.

Building as an ordinary business

The finance that banks supply to builders for estate development is working capital. Although the assets being financed are land and buildings, they are not for the business's own use and cannot therefore be classified as capital expenditure. Such advances do, however, meet my definition of working capital in that they are necessary to 'oil the wheels' of the business.

In an 'ordinary' business, a bank working capital facility would finance debtors and stock. A speculative builder has very few debtors. Debtors will usually arise only through house sales where contracts have been exchanged and completion monies are due within, usually, 28 days. The finance is mainly therefore used to fund stock. The stock of a builder can be broken down as follows:

Raw material   – Land

Work in progress   – Houses in course of construction

Finished goods   – Completed houses.

A bank would always prefer to finance debtors rather than stock. This is partly because debtors are more liquid – by definition, in most businesses debtors turn into cash more quickly than stock can. It is also the case that stock breaks up worse than debtors in a liquidation. This is particularly true of work in progress, and in building advances work in progress is always a big element of a lender's security. So, on the face of it, a logical lender should be very wary of lending working capital finance to builders.

Why, then, are banks prepared to lend more to builders than they normally would to a manufacturing business? Why can 200% gearing be acceptable, or 2:1 lending against the business's stake in a project? I believe the reasons are:

(a) It is possible to obtain a fixed charge over the 'stock', and because this stock can only be sold under carefully controlled conditions, it is relatively easy to control. The security is 'good'.

(b) Because the stock has to be in one particular place, it is possible through site visits and in other ways to closely monitor the fact that the funds provided to cover work in progress do in fact add to the value of the security and are not diverted, for example, to repay creditors.

(c)   There is the capacity to establish independently by using, for example, local estate agents, the state of the market for the stock and the saleability and sales prospects for individual items of stock, such as houses.

Many people would regard the first of these reasons as being the most important. Having good security is always a great comfort for a lender, but it must always be remembered that the important thing about looking at security is to have a good view of its cash value on realization.

The second reason is essentially a corollary of the first in that it is about maintaining security values in relation to the lending. In practice, it is very difficult to form a clear view of what a building development would realise if it had to be sold before completion. Similarly, it is difficult to predict what virgin land with planning permission will realise. The reason why a building company is likely to get into difficulties is that houses are not selling, and against the background of a difficult market place all bets tend to be off with regard to security values. This is why the third reason is so important and should form an absolute prerequisite for the adoption of the usually quoted building advance formulae.

High gearing is tolerable only when a business has a strong and reliable cash flow. In its absence the risk is high that a business may not be able to meet interest and may have unexpected or unwelcome demands to borrow more to meet creditors, and so on. So, if a steady sales income is denied to a builder because the national or local housing market has poor prospects, then the 'usual formulae' cannot be applied. Similarly, if there is a particularly strong and certain cash flow, a more relaxed view can be taken. This means that building is no different from any other business, and the efforts of the lender need to be directed to looking at the certainty of cash flow to cover repayment as the crucial aspect of the credit assessment.

Building advance cash flow forecastIng

Two aspects of a building company's cash flow need to be subject to careful scrutiny, and essentially two types of forecast should be produced:

(a)   an overall cash flow forecast for the business;

(b)   a detailed forecast for the individual developments to be undertaken.

The overall forecast is needed to ensure a continuing perspective on all the cash demands and general cash-generating capacity of the business as a whole. This will demonstrate whether the company can meet its obligations to provide its cash stake in particular developments, and whether there is a surplus to meet unexpected contingencies. The overall cash flow will be an amalgamation of the individual development cash flows, which will need to go into the detailed inflows and outflows in relation to particular sites.

Both types of cash flow need to be rigorously tested to ensure that the assumptions built into them are correct. This is particularly true for the individual development cash flows, and the factors that should be taken into account when examining a development are fully set out in Chapter 10 of *Bankers' Lending Techniques*.

The major factor, which cannot be emphasized too strongly, is that no matter how strong the security, the lender must be satisfied that the borrower has an ongoing business that can repay the borrowing according to plan.

Case 1

Jack Russell and his brother Martin are builders and have been customers at your branch for several years. Jack started as a bricklayer and after several years became a foreman. His brother is a qualified quantity surveyor. Seven years ago they decided to form their own business, Supa Homes Ltd.

The business has provided a fair living due mainly to the directors' capacity for hard work and their spending as much time as possible on site. Work done includes 'small works' contracts, alterations, extensions, refurbishment and some 'new build' contracts for private customers and small developers. In the last 12 months they have also built two large detached houses on the remainder of the land purchased for their own properties, and one is contracted for sale at £80,000 to the local manager of a competitor bank. The other is almost complete and, at a price of £90,000, there are several people interested in purchasing it.

The Russells tend to be rather demanding customers, and have called to advise you that they have been successful at auction in purchasing an old house, which has sufficient land attached for two pairs of semi-detached properties. They request an increase of £200,000 in the limit. This increase is calculated as follows:

	£
Purchase of house and land	101,500
Building cost of four semi-detached houses	75,000
Renovation of old house	15,000
Services	10,000
	201,500

	£
Repayments from sales	
Old detached house	75,000
Four semi-detached houses @ £45,000	180,000
	255,000

The present limit on the account is £50,000, which is fully utilized. Balance sheets for the last three years are already in your possession.

This is a typical small housebuilder situation with a requirement to lend for the next development before the existing development has been completed. An analysis of the proposition shows how inappropriate it may be to depend on the usual building advance formulae to determine the level of borrowing.

The business is well established and has a proven track record. The management is experienced and is unusual for a small builder in that Martin Russell is professionally qualified. The historical financial information shows a sound company, with gearing at the various balance sheet dates not having been much more than 50%, and with a steadily increasing net margin. Retentions have been good, as shown in the increased capital base. The switch from contracting to speculative building seems to have been a success.

The brothers have been somewhat impetuous in purchasing the old house at auction without having their finance arranged, and this should cause some concern. However, given their track record, the bank ought to be able to help. In this instance, given the small size of the company, a special cash flow forecast for the new site is probably not appropriate and a simple overall cash flow forecast should suffice. It would be interesting to know how their contract debtors stand and what creditors are due but, given the position shown in the historical balance sheets, it is fair to assume that there will be more debtor money to collect than creditors to pay.

SUPA HOMES LTD
BALANCE SHEETS

As at 31 December	Year A £	Year A £	Year B £	Year B £	Year C £	Year C £
Fixed assets						
Plant and machinery	15,900		26,800		28,200	
Vehicles	5,000	20,900	9,000	35,800	9,500	37,700
Current assets						
Debtors	57,400		53,200		56,500	
Land	18,100		18,100		18,100	
Work in progress	54,500	130,000	53,400	124,700	96,400	171,000
		150,900		160,500		208,700
Current liabilities						
Creditors	45,100		36,400		35,500	
Tax	4,700		11,900		12,300	
Hire purchase	3,200		6,900		4,500	
Bank	31,000	84,000	18,000	73,200	47,600	99,900
		66,900		87,300		108,800
Represented by:						
Issued share capital		1,000		1,000		1,000
Profit and loss account		65,900		86,300		107,800
		66,900		87,300		108,800
Pretax profit		16,600		31,300		34,800
After charging:						
Depreciation	8,200		6,400		9,500	
Interest	4,400		3,300		8,600	
Directors' remuneration	12,400		15,800		19,200	
Audit fees	300		400		500	
	25 300		25,900		37,800	
Tax payable		4,200		10,900		13,300
Retained profit		12,400		20,400		21,500
Sales		310,000		417,000		390,000

ACCOUNTING RATIOS

	Year A	Year B	Year C
Gearing (%)	51	29	49
Net margin (%)	5.3	7.5	8.9

A simple cash flow forecast would show the following position:

	£
Present borrowing	50,000
Purchase of land	101,500
	151,500
Sale proceeds of contracted sale (assuming 10% already received)	72,000
	79,500
Building etc. costs	100,000
	179,500
Sale proceeds of house sold subject to contract	90,000
	89,500
Sale proceeds of houses to be built etc.	255,000
Surplus (before interest)	165,500

The requested limit of £200,000 would imply 200% gearing but it can be seen that the borrowing will never reach anything like that level. The maximum borrowing in the cash flow forecast is £179,500, and although this does not include interest or overheads, the proceeds of the house sold subject to contract, and perhaps also the old detached house, could be received far in advance of the full drawdown to meet building costs. A simple understanding of the anticipated funds flow through the business in relation to the old and new developments is all that is required.

The development appears to be profitable on the figures shown, generating a 20% return. Obviously, it will still be necessary to confirm the saleability of the properties and their pricing. Ideally, the pricing should be confirmed by independent professionals. To ensure that the properties can be sold easily, Supa Homes Ltd should be registered with the NHBC, and this and other items of detail, such as seeing copies of planning permission and so on, will need to be investigated.

Provided all these things are in order, there should be no problem in agreeing the requested limit, which can be expected to reduce quite quickly to below £100,000.

Case 2

Fred Mix is 65 years old. He and his son Wayne, aged 35, are directors of F. Mix & Son (Building Contractors) Ltd, a long-established firm of contracting builders. The company has had its account with your bank for over 20 years. In recent years Fred has been handing over the reins of the business to Wayne and has also gradually been transferring control so that now Wayne owns 75% of the shares in the company.

The company has traditionally carried out contracting work only, mainly for local authorities and private developers. During the past 12 months it has been building houses on a site owned by a local property company.

You have in the past allowed overdrafts up to £200,000, secured by Fred and Wayne's unlimited guarantees, which have been supported by a first charge over Fred's house, valued at £250,000, and a second charge over Wayne's house, which has an equity of £75,000.

Fred and Wayne call to see you. They tell you of two major changes that they have decided to make, which will affect both the business and the bank. These are:

(a) Fred is retiring from active participation in the company. He will be selling his house in England and plans to live in Portugal. He will be retaining his existing shareholding but will be resigning as a director. He now requests you to release him from both his guarantee and the charge over his house.

(b) Wayne wishes to move the company away from its traditional contracting business and into speculative housebuilding. Present contracts are nearly complete and he has deliberately not been entering into new ones. The company has the opportunity to buy 1½ acres of land in a nearby village, which has outline planning permission for 10 small detached houses. Wayne has prepared a cash flow forecast for the project, which shows a need for an overdraft of £450,000. He requests that you lend the company this sum.

Here we have a contracting building company going into speculative building for the first time. Although there are apparently two separate requests from the directors, in practice they are closely related.

While some analysis of the historical accounts is obviously necessary, it needs to be appreciated that the planned change in the nature of the business would also completely change the asset structure of the balance sheet, and it is the future scenario that has to be considered. Before the request to release Fred Mix's security can be agreed, an assessment has to be made of the viability of the proposed change of course set out in the second request.

The projections for the proposed development show the full cost, and the bank would not be prepared to lend 100% in this situation. Using the most liberal of the different building advance formulae – one-third/two-thirds – the bank could lend £200,000 towards the £300,000 cost of the land and £100,000 of the total peak building costs of £150,000. Thus the business would have to find £150,000 from its own resources by the cash flow peak. The most crucial issue in the proposition must be to determine whether the company can in fact do this.

The management accounts as at the end of March show a total of debtors and cash of £261,000. Given the run-down in contracting, this ought to be available to provide the company's cash stake by the commencement of the development.

In due course, some of the retention monies would also be released. An overall corporate cash flow for the business needs to be seen so that it can be formally established that sufficient funds would be available to meet creditors as well as the stake in the project.

The assumptions underlying the development projection need to be considered and tested:

(a) Are the selling prices of the houses in line with the market?

(b) The first sales completion is not planned to take place until month 6 – this appears to be conservative.

(c) Constant building costs have been assumed through the development – again conservative, as the heavier costs in building a house tend to come at the end, approximately 45% after a property is roofed in.

(d) The building costs per square foot need to be judged against industry norms.

(e) The way the revenue is forecast suggests that the company will be completing two houses at a time and, after the company has provided its cash stake, it should be possible for the bank to be repaid well before the end of the development.

F. MIX & SON (BUILDING CONTRACTORS) LTD
BALANCE SHEETS

	Audited accounts 30 September Year A		Management accounts 31 March Year B	
	£000	£000	£000	£000
Current assets				
Cash	–		105	
Retentions	36		30	
Debtors	101		156	
Stock	29		23	
Work in progress	307	473	70	384
Current liabilities				
Creditors	92		101	
Hire purchase	54		43	
Bank overdraft	126			
Tax	54	326	34	178
Net current assets		147		206
Fixed assets				
Leasehold improvements	23		21	
Plant and machinery	40		32	
Vehicles	35	98	27	80
Net assets		245		286
Financed by:				
Ordinary shares		10		10
Profit and loss		235		276
		245		286

PROFIT AND LOSS ACCOUNT SUMMARY

	12 months to 30 Sept. Year A £000	6 months to 31 March Year B £000
Turnover	2,086	1,012
Gross profit	213	111
Net profit before tax	98	41

MONTHLY CASH FLOW

Month	Land	Building	Selling fees	Sales revenue	Cumulative capital employed	Assumed interest at 15%
	£	£	£	£	£	£
1	304,200		·		(304,200)	
2		37,625			(341,825)	
3		37,625			(379,450)	13,000
4		37,625			(417,075)	
5		37,625		16,000	(438,700)	
6		37,625	2,600	160,000	(318,925)	15,000
7		37,625	2,600	160,000	(199,150)	
8		37,625	2,600	160,000	(79,375)	
9		37,625	2,600	160,000	40,400	3,000
10			2,600	144,000	181,800	
	£304,200	£301,000	£13,000	£800,000		£31,000

The profitability of the development must also be tested, but some simple outline figures show that this should be the case:

	£	£
Sales revenue		800,000
Less: Land cost	304,200	
Building costs	301,000	
Selling costs	13,000	618,200
		181,800
Less: Interest (say 2/3 of £31,000)		20,700
Profit		161,100

A professional valuation of the land would be needed, and ideally the lending would take place against architects' certificates at agreed stages. Given that the bank should be able to obtain 150% security cover by land and work in progress (because of the amount of cash the company can inject), the security arrangements are probably acceptable, provided it can be established – again, ideally, through outside professional advice – that the houses will be readily saleable.

The lending needs to be on a loan account, rather than overdraft, to ensure that the bank can control the position.

Provided the necessary questions can be answered satisfactorily, a total lending of £300,000 for the development does not look unreasonable, and as adequate security cover can be found within the development, backed up by the second charge on Wayne Mix's house, then Fred Mix's guarantee and the charge over his house could be released.

Keyman insurance over Wayne Mix's life is necessary, and all the usual technical issues, such as site and planning permission and confirmation that the houses will have NHBC certificates, will need to be tied up.

Case 3

Castle Builders Ltd is a firm of speculative housebuilders. The company was established 18 years ago and has a good reputation for building quality houses in your area. It currently finances its building developments through two of your local competitor banks. For some time you have being trying to persuade Castle's directors to give you some of their business.

You now receive a letter from Castle's Finance Director. In it he tells you that the company is part-way through the development of four sites. Unexpectedly, it has the opportunity to buy 2 acres of land with outline planning permission to erect eight four-bedroomed detached houses from another local builder who is in financial difficulties. With his letter he includes some extracts from the company's latest management accounts and an outline feasibility study for developing the new site. He asks on what terms you would be prepared to finance the development of the new site.

This is a long-established firm of builders with a good track record, and the bank has been pushing for the business. However, as yet no formal analysis of the company has been undertaken, and particular care is needed because it is multi-banked. The prospect exists that any lending one makes might easily end up as work in progress on another site to the benefit of another bank's security.

CASTLE BUILDERS LTD
BALANCE SHEET

	£000	£000
Fixed assets		
Land and buildings	150	
Plant and machinery	322	472
Current assets		
Development land and work in progress	1,868	
Trade debtors		
Other debtors	3	
Cash	686	2,558
Current liabilities		
Bank loans	1,239	
Trade creditors	1,065	
Other creditors	2	
Tax	134	(2,440)
Net tangible assets		590
Financed by:		
Share capital		100
Profit and loss account		490
		590

PROFIT AND LOSS SUMMARY

Previous 12 months	£000
Sales	5,163
Gross profit	444
Interest payable	Nil
Profit before tax	72

RATIOS

Gross margin (%)	8.6
Net margin (%)	0.01
Net gearing (%)	94

FEASIBILITY STUDY FIGURES

	£
Costings	
Purchase of land	500,000
Building costs	240,000
Drains	20,000
Roads	32,000
Services	10,000
Building, planning and NHBC fees	4,000
Solicitors and estate agents	15,000
Contingency	1 5,000
	836,000
Sale proceeds	
8 houses at £135,000 each	1,080,000
Anticipated profit (before interest)	244,000 (22.6%)

The projections show the full development, but the bank would not wish to lend 100%. If a one-third/two-thirds basis was adopted, the bank would lend £333,000 towards the cost of land (£500,000) and £224,000 towards the cost of building (£336,000). In addition, there would be the possibility of having to roll up interest pending sales, so total limits of around £600,000 would be required. The company would have to find £300,000 itself, although the latest management accounts suggest that far more than this is readily available. However, some caution is needed and a full corporate cash flow is required because, despite the high cash balances, creditors are also substantial and cannot easily be met from the available liquid resources. It will obviously be important to establish how quickly existing land and work in progress will turn into cash. A full report on the saleability of the houses on existing sites will be needed, and it will also be appropriate to establish the size of other bank facilities to ensure that the company's overall borrowing needs can be met.

The proposed development appears to be profitable but, as in the previous case, the projections need to be tested. The estimated profit is well above the gross margin in the management accounts – 22.6% compared with 8.6%. However, it may be unrealistic to compare this margin with that in the profit and loss account; work done in the last 12 months may not yet have come through in sales. If this were so, the profits in the management accounts would be understated. More information is needed.

Are the selling prices for the houses in line with the market, and can we have a professional opinion? Are the building costs per square foot in line with industry norms, and is the price being paid for the land reasonable? Moreover, the feasibility study does not give any indication of the phasing of cash flows, and a cash flow projection for the development will be needed to clarify the position.

Provided the various questions can be answered satisfactorily, a 150% security cover by land and work in progress ought to be available. Close control will need to be exercised – lending against architects' certificates at agreed stages would be appropriate. It will be particularly important that the monitoring arrangements are tight in this instance because of the multi-bank situation.

This is a proposition worth exploring, but there is as yet insufficient information to reach any firm conclusion. With the multi-banked situation and an apparently tight liquidity position, there is a need for a great deal of caution. Any refusal to provide the extra information or to structure the lending in the way the bank needs ought to result in a refusal to lend.

6

Property lending

In recent years banks have probably made more mistakes lending on property than any other single type of borrowing. The lending tap gets turned on in the good times with reasonably strict parameters, which then get relaxed as the market place becomes more aggressive, and the whole thing ends in tears as oversupply of property meets economic downturn causing reduced demand. The cyclical nature of the property market is plain to see in any history of banking in the 1970s, 1980s and 1990s.

Banks have reacted to this situation in all sorts of ways. Some have restricted property lending to specialist units, some have imposed sectoral caps, and some have tried to withdraw from the business altogether. There are difficulties with all these approaches. Specialist units need to do business to justify their cost and existence. They can become over-convinced of their own expertise and ability to 'beat the market'. Caps and withdrawal often punish the better borrowers more than the bad. This is because poorer credits by definition are hard to get repaid and stick in the portfolio, while the better lendings reduce and take the strain of restrictive policies that prevent them being re-drawn.

There is a need to pick winners in the property business. This sounds – and is – fraught with danger. There are long lead times in property development and a lot of inflexibility in repayment plans linked to the performance of a few – often one – assets. One approach that does not work is trying to guess the trend of the property cycle. Bankers are notoriously bad at this. They are amateurs swimming in a pool full of sharks, who are only too willing to take advantage of any sign of weakness. So, how can this be done?

In my opinion, the answer is to get away from the notion that property lending is a type of asset finance where the present and future value of the asset is key. The top-quality property men think mainly in terms of managing the cash flows involved in a property. The lending will be repaid from cash flow, so this is the aspect on which we must focus rather than the property's value at any point in time.

Of course it would be naïve to think that it is possible to dissociate value from cash flow. The true value of any asset is the net present value of its future cash flows. But this is a theoretical point, and concentrating on the cash inflows and outflows associated with a property is as much about approaching propositions with the right state of mind and technique as anything else.

The cash flow approach focuses attention on the certainty and reliability of the cash arriving or flowing out, the time scales involved, and the margins for error. The margins for error are a key portion of the risk assessment, and using the cash flow approach readily identifies the areas where sensitivity analysis is necessary and possible. It also enables the proposition to be reduced to 'bite size' pieces where common sense assumptions of changes in market or other conditions can be applied.

The cash flows in property transactions are easily identified. They are:

(a) the purchase cost;

(b) the end sale price;

(c) the borrower's stake in the transaction;

(d) one-off costs such as the cost of construction or legal and other costs in relation to the purchase or sale;

(e) continuing costs such as maintenance, insurance and property taxes;

(f) interest on any borrowing;

(g) income from rents if let.

This list covers the main areas but is not exhaustive. There may be unusual costs that relate to specific deals, but the overall approach is clear.

Types of property transaction

There are two main types of property transaction, and the case studies in this chapter will look at one of each.

They are:

(a) *Property investment* – This is lending provided to purchase an existing property, with repayment coming from the rental income of the property.

(b) *Property development* – This is, in effect, bridging finance to enable the borrower to purchase and develop the land or property with repayment coming from its sale.

Some propositions may be combinations of the two with the completed building being let, but ownership being retained by the developer as an investment. In such a case the development bridging finance might be repaid by re-financing through a term loan. Where this occurs, the lending techniques for both types of transaction need to be applied together.

Property investment

The borrower will have identified an attractive investment opportunity in a property. This could take the form of a good potential income yield or capital gain, or a combination of the two. Indeed, a growth in income will be the main driver of capital gain.

What are the cash flows and how should they be assessed?

(a) The purchase cost should be relatively certain, although if a deal has not actually been firmly agreed, the possibility of an increase in the price (and/or a reduction) should be built into the sensitivity analysis.

(b) The end sale price is not known and may not even be relevant if the proposition is easily repaid from income from the property. A lender will not want to be dependent on future capital appreciation, however likely this may seem, for any element of repayment. If the proceeds of eventual sale are to be part of the repayment proposal, then conservative assumptions are going to be necessary as this event is likely to be a long way into the future and market value is likely to be difficult to predict. A key consideration will be the location of the property and its versatility of use that is, all those things that affect its ease of marketability. It is likely that the property will be sold to an investor who will be interested mainly in the likely investment yield to be expected. Knowing the types of yield required by investors on similar properties will help the sale value calculation, although it has to be acknowledged that the required yields will fluctuate with market sentiment and the return on other less risky investments.

(c) The borrower's stake ought theoretically to be certain, and the proposition ideally should be structured to ensure this is made the case by its going in first. However, in the real world a borrower's stake may be coming from the sale proceeds of another transaction. If this represents a closed bridge of another asset sale, this may be acceptable; otherwise the high degree of uncertainty involved is likely to make the proposition unattractive.

(d) The one-off costs will include legal costs, stamp duty, VAT in some cases, survey costs and the cost of any refurbishment necessary. It ought to be possible to predict these with some certainty.

(e) There will be continuing costs in managing the property because collection of rents and the administration will involve cost. Most landlords, however seek to pass on as many of the continuing costs of a property to the tenants through clauses in their leases which are often described as 'full repairing and insuring' leases. These also ensure that the costs of property taxes and regular maintenance are paid by the tenants.

Where this is not the case – most often with furnished residential property – allowance must be made for the expenditure when assessing the extent to which income is available to meet debt-servicing costs. The devil is in the detail here, and a close understanding of the individual lease terms is essential.

(f) The interest on the borrowing will need to be sensitized for changes in fluctuating rates. If the rate can be fixed then of course there is more certainty in the cash flows. The amount of capital reduction required by the lender can be added to the interest to produce a cash flow figure that is generally referred to as the debt service amount, which can then be expressed as a ratio in relation to rental income.

(g) The availability of income from rents is almost certain to be the most crucial issue in the transaction because the maintenance of adequate debt/service cover is going to be key for the lender. Anything that makes the income uncertain or creates a potential shortfall must be bad. The main considerations are:

(i) *Terms of leases* – Where possible the lease term should be longer than the term of the lending. If this is not so, there could be void periods where there is no income from tenants, which will have to be factored into the rental income cash flow assumptions.

(ii) *Quality of tenants* – This is really about whether the tenants are creditworthy to meet their obligations under the lease. If there are are doubts about this the rental cash flow assumption must be sensitized accordingly.

Despite a concentration on cash flow, it would be naïve to ignore security value altogether. In fact the security margin provides an essential 'sanity check' on the sensitivities in the cash flow analysis. We have said above that theoretically the value of a property is the net present values of its future cash flows. The security margin therefore needs to cover the worst case position as identified by the cash flow sensitivity analysis. The degree of certainty in cash flow will determine this, although it is interesting to note that historical experience has led bankers to look for around 150%.

Maintenance of an adequate cash flow from the property to service capital and interest should be included as a debt service covenant. The maintenance of an adequate security margin based on regular valuations should also be a standard covenant.

As well as taking a charge over the property, the bank should also take a simple floating charge. The reason for this is that under the terms of present insolvency legislation another creditor could secure the appointment of an administrator, who would then control the rental income needed to repay the bank. The ability to appoint an administrative receiver under a floating charge defeats this.

Property development

As stated above, lending for property development is a kind of bridging finance. There will be a number of uncertainties affecting the cash flows, and the key to lending successfully is to eliminate these as far as possible by creating something as close to a closed bridge as is practicable.

The issues impacting on the cash flows are as follows:-

(a)   The purchase cost ought to be known and the one-off costs such as legal expenses and stamp duty easy to estimate. The purchase cost will be heavily influenced by whether the property already holds planning permission for the development. Ideally, the property should have detailed planning permission for the precise type of development proposed. If only outline planning permission is held, or the construction plan envisages getting changes to the existing permission, then these uncertainties should be factored into the sensitivity analysis.

A full survey of the property ought to be undertaken, with particular attention being paid to potential environmental risk, which could add significantly to construction costs.

(b)   The end sale price will have to be based on the best estimate of what the property will be worth in its finished state. Professional advice from a reliable estate agent with good knowledge of the area and type of property involved should be obtained. Ideally, the property should be pre-sold to a buyer who is creditworthy enough to complete the transaction so repayment is dependent only on building work being successfully completed. In the absence of a watertight contract and/or creditworthy buyer, appropriate sensitivity analysis will be required.

(c)   The borrower's stake should go in first to make it certain, but many developers rely on the sale of other properties to provide their stake as they will need to acquire land well in advance of construction beginning in order to maintain a steady flow of work. The certainty of the arrival of sale proceeds from sales of other properties may have to be assessed.

(d)   The major one-off cost is that of construction of the building. Ideally a fixed-price building contract would be negotiated but these are now rare. A good contract builder will seek to pass on the additional costs of rises in the price of materials etc. Sufficient contingency must be built into the estimates to cover potential cost overruns.

The financial viability of the builder will be vital. If the builder were to fail during the construction period then the extra cost involved in finding a new builder and the cost of the time lost would be considerable. Full enquiries into the viability of the builder must be made. It is imperative to ensure that the money lent for construction is actually spent on the building and not diverted elsewhere. Independent inspection of the work done and control of drawdown in accordance with reports from architects or quantity surveyors is necessary for tight control.

(e)   If the transaction is successful, there ought not to be any continuing costs because the property will be sold immediately. Continuing costs such as insurance, security, maintenance and perhaps property taxes (these may not be payable or payable at a lower rate if a property is empty) will need to be considered if a buyer is not likely to acquire it on completion of the construction.

(f)   Interest will usually be rolled up during the construction phase of a development simply because there is no cash flow to meet it until a sale is achieved. The lender will need to be satisfied there is sufficient profit margin in the overall transaction to meet this in all possible circumstances. The time it will take to sell the property will be the key element here.

(g)   Usually there will be no income from a property development transaction until it is sold. Income considerations would arise only if an empty property was let temporarily pending sale.

It goes without saying that the property should be taken as security to control the advance. It is also usually appropriate to take a simple floating charge to enable the bank to appoint an administrative receiver to complete a half-finished project.

Case 1

. . . .

Grant Anderson is a 35-year-old qualified accountant who has banked with you for 18 years. He practises in partnership with another accountant, Arthur Thornton, aged 34, as Anderson & Thornton Chartered Accountants. The partnership banks with you, maintaining useful credit balances on both office and clients' accounts.

Five years ago the partners established a property company called Anderson & Thornton Properties Limited, each holding 50% of the shares. This company owns two freehold retail units in one of the better-quality London suburbs. These were purchased at a cost of £426,000 with the assistance of a £300,000 25-year mortgage loan from a foreign bank. Both units are let on 30-year leases, which have 24 years to run, and following a five-yearly rent review last year, gross rental income amounts to £76,000 per annum.

The property company also banks at your branch but there is little activity on the account as it is used mainly for the receipt of rents and to make the mortgage payments to the foreign bank.

Anderson calls to see you. The property company wishes to buy two more freehold retail units, which will cost £200,000 each. One has an annual income of £16,000 and the other £20,000. The leases on the properties both have over 30 years to run and contain provisions for seven-year rent reviews. The next reviews are due in 15 months and 18 months respectively. Anderson gives you a copy of the latest audited accounts. He asks you to grant the company a bridging loan of £400,000 for two years, after which he will refinance the properties on a long-term mortgage.

ANDERSON & THORNTON PROPERTIES LIMITED
BALANCE SHEET

As at 31 December	Year A £	£	Year B £	£
Current assets				
Cash	13,860		7,008	
Debtors and payments	11,004	24,864	19,496	26,504
Current liabilities				
Credits	3,556		5,230	
Tax	2,166	(5,722)	2,166	(7,396)
		19,142		19,108
Fixed assets				
Freehold property	426,000		760,000	
Plant and equipment	546	426,546	464	760,464
Total assets:		445,688		779,572
Financed by				
Long-term loan		291,276		283,538
Issued share capital	126,000		126,000	
Capital reserve	–		334,000	
Profit and loss account	28,412	154,412	36,034	496,034
		445,688		779,572

PROFIT AND LOSS SUMMARY

12 months to 31 December	Year A £	Year B £
Gross income	42,6000	61,500
Interest	35,280	34,320
Directors' remuneration	3,080	19,900
Profit before tax	3,060	4,440

ACCOUNTING RATIOS

	Year A	Year B
Net gearing(%)	180	56
Interest cover (times)	1.09	1.13
Net margin (%)	7.2	7.2

This is a good long-standing relationship with a pair of young professionals, and the bank would wish to help. However, the 100% amount and two-year period of the proposed bridging loan are uncomfortable. They are needed because the rationale underlying the request is to carry the business past the next rent reviews. The partners are hoping for increases in rents to increase the cash flows and raise the investment value to enable re-financing to take place in two years' time.

The balance sheet indicates that the present properties have already been revalued on the back of increased rental income. The business has limited cash, with surplus income siphoned off as increased directors' remuneration. In fact the balance sheet is a very simple document, with current assets and liabilities presumably reflecting delayed rental receipts and expense payments. The small amount of cash would on its own be insufficient to meet the one-off legal costs etc. involved in the property purchases. However, with the surplus rents, the business is cash generative, and cash from debtor collection ought to be enough to meet these costs.

Gearing has reduced as a direct consequence of the property revaluation. But gearing will increase to around 136% if the new facility is agreed.

Is there sufficient cash flow to make the proposition viable? Interest on £400,000 at say 11% would be £44,000 compared with rental income of only £36,000. However, there are surplus rents from the current properties available. Repayments on the 25-year £300,000 mortgage at 11% would be £35,028 per annum compared with annual rental income of £76,000 – a surplus of over £40,000. On paper this looks to be sufficient, but a detailed budget of continuing expenses should be provided to establish what expenses have to be paid out of gross rents.

The quality of the tenants must be tested using bank status enquiries. The stability of rental cash flow is vital, and any potential void periods would be damaging to viability.

The source of repayment is not firm. Institutions prepared to re-finance this type of transaction certainly exist, but a long-term lender would want a minimum debt service cover ratio of at least 100% and would probably also want to lend no more than 70% of an independent valuation. There can be no guarantee that the rents will increase to a sufficient degree.

Re-financing is too uncertain to make the proposition viable. Could the deal be re-engineered to improve it? It looks possible to include some interim capital repayment of the bridging loan from surplus rents: £70,000 over the two years looks possible. This would still leave things tight, and the directors should be asked to re-inject some of the cash they have taken out: £20,000 ought to be enough. First charges on the new properties and second charges over the existing properties plus a simple debenture should be taken.

Case 2

Stephen Linley is a successful property developer who has banked with you for over 25 years. He is 59 years old, and is believed to have a personal net worth in excess of £30 million.

Linley calls to see you. He has a new property development project planned and wants to give your bank the opportunity to provide the necessary funding. He has found a site with planning permission for 40,000 square feet of offices, which he can acquire for £2 million. He is convinced that once he owns the site he will be able to get the planning permission altered to allow 50,000 square feet, which he believes will immediately increase the value to £2.8 million.

He is establishing a brand new company to carry out the transaction. Its initial share capital will be the £2 million that will be used to buy the site; the company will then seek to borrow the remaining funds needed to complete the building. Linley has produced a project appraisal, which he gives to you. Construction will not begin until the enhanced planning permission has been granted. He is seeking a loan of up to £5.3 million for up to two years three months to complete the development.

Repayment is to come from the sale of the completed development to an institutional buyer. Linley has two pension funds and an insurance company interested in acquiring the building when it is fully let. Two major international companies have expressed a keen interest in taking all the office space when built.

Linley asks for a loan of £5.3 million from the bank.

PROJECT APPRAISAL

Sales

Rent: net usable space 50,000 sq. ft @ £15 per sq. ft = £750,000

	£
Income capitalised at 7% yield	10,714,285
Less 2.75% purchasers' costs	295,643
Sales value	10,418,642

Costs

	£	£
Site cost	2,000,000	
Stamp duty on site @ 1%	20,000	
Legal fees on site @ 0.5%	10,000	
Agents' fees on site @ 1%	20,000	
Total site costs		2,050,000
Building 50,000 sq. ft @ £60 per sq. ft	3,000,000	
Access roads	750,000	
Site clearance	50,000	
Contingency @ 2.5%	95,000	
Professional fees @ 12%	456,000	
Total building costs		4,351,000
Interest @ 9.5% (10% APR)		
Site acquisition costs (15 months to end of building)	5,475	
Construction and fees (12 months averaged)	217,500	
Void period (complete but empty – 12 months)	440,100	
Total interest costs		663,075
Agents' letting fees @ 15% of rent	112,500	
Legal fees on letting @ 1%	7,500	
Agents' capital sale fees @ 0.5%	52,093	
Advertising and promotion costs	30,000	
Total disposal and end costs		202,093
Total costs		7,266,168

	£	
Sales value	10,418,642	
Less: total costs	7,266,168	
Profit	3,152,474	(Profit on cost 43.4%)

Linley is a good customer whom the bank would want to help. His track record suggests that he knows the business, but it has to be said that plenty of experienced property men have got this marketplace wrong.

Despite the indications about future tenants etc., the development is neither pre-sold nor pre-let, and so is open ended and speculative. Moreover, by forming a new company, Linley keeps the risk in this transaction away from the companies that contain his wealth. The bank cannot look to assets outside the development if things go wrong.

Linley is putting a good stake, £2 million, into the project, so he has plenty at risk. Even so, gearing will be high at 265%. Rolling up interest is not ideal but is probably acceptable if all else stacks up.

Theoretically, there is a wide margin in the transaction if all the assumptions are right. The bank gets out if the property sells for £5.3 million within 2 years 3 months, compared with the proposed sale value of £10.4 million. But there are a number of risks:

Letting risk:

(a)   It might not be possible to let the building at all if the market is depressed.

(b)   The interest from the two large companies is a positive sign, but there is a big difference between interest and a legal tenancy agreement.

(c)   What competitive space of a similar quality is available in the area?

(d)   It could well be that letting will not be achieved until the building is complete, and the market could be different then.

(e)   The rent of £15 per square foot might not be achievable. Is there an independent view of local rents available?

(f)   The 12-month void period looks a conservative assumption, but if it is exceeded, additional interest costs will eat into the profit margin at the same time as there will be pressure to reduce the rent.

(g)   The quality of the tenants will be an important issue for any acquiring institution.

Construction risk:

(a) Building costs could overrun the estimates. Will there be a fixed-price building contract?

(b) There is a need to ensure the builder is reputable and can fulfil the contract. Linley is experienced and ought to get this right.

(c) The 2.5% contingency will cover only minor mishaps.

Disposal risk:

(a) The interest from the institutions is positive but is dependent on pre-letting and presumably tenant quality, so it could easily not come to fruition.

(b) If there is a delay in letting, then institutional appetite could fade.

(c) Alternatively the institutions might require a better yield than 7%.

(d) If this happened, the sale value would fall, probably significantly.

Despite the apparent good margin in the transaction, it remains entirely speculative, and most banks would not be prepared to take the risk. The key is for the building to be pre-let, then, given the good customer stake, the proposition should be acceptable. A first charge over the property would be required as well as a simple debenture. Drawdown should be against quantity surveyor's or architect's certificates.

Professionals

All banks seek the business of professional people. They represent potentially very wealthy personal customers but, more importantly, are very influential in terms of gaining new business. They act as advisors to business and personal customers, and many of them handle large amounts of clients' monies, which can provide a useful source of credit balances to banks.

A wide range of people consider themselves professionals, but the normal distinguishing feature is that a professional is usually self-employed and provides a service for a fee rather than buying and selling something. This definition does not fit every circumstance: doctors working in the National Health Service, for example, are generally accepted as professionals, although historically this is probably due more to the fact that many doctors do private work for fees.

The best-quality professionals have restricted and highly regulated entry qualifications to their professions. There will usually be stiff examination requirements, and a professional qualification will be needed as a 'licence to practise'. This restriction on entry has enabled some professional bodies to regulate the supply of their services to the marketplace to keep the income of their members high and stable. Increasingly, professional bodies are having to justify restrictive practices. Competition is developing in all professions, with much more advertising taking place, and a willingness by potential clients to shop around to get the best deal on cost. It is probably the case that professionals generally are not going to have as easy a time in the future as they have had in the past, and are going to have to act much more like ordinary businessmen, with all the implications this has for credit-assessing their businesses.

From a banker's point of view, professions can be looked at in two groups:

(a) those that are influential in introducing new business, for example accountants, solicitors, estate agents, and so on;

(b) those who will not be a source of new business except for themselves, for example doctors, dentists, architects.

Legal and accounting issues

While most business customers that a bank deals with are limited companies or sole traders, professionals tend to come together in partnerships. Some operate on their own as sole traders, and it is possible for some professionals to trade as limited companies, but the partnership is the norm.

In England (though not in Scotland) a 'firm' has no separate personality that can be distinguished from the personalities of the individuals composing the partnership. A contract with a company is not an agreement with an individual member but with the 'person' that the company is in a legal sense. A contract with a partnership on the other hand is a contract with all the individuals composing the firm.

The liability of partners towards the creditors of a firm is joint. Bankers always insist on a joint and several mandate from partners to ensure that each partner is individually liable for all partnership debts to the bank, as well as the firm jointly. This means that all the partners' personal assets are available to meet a firm's debts, so there is no need for separate guarantees as would be the case with a company and its directors.

Normally, partners draw up a document termed a partnership agreement, which defines their rights and duties. It is not essential that this agreement be evidenced in writing, but ideally it is. If there is no formal agreement, the Partnership Act 1890 lays down the rules that will apply, including the fact that all partners will share equally in capital profits and losses and that they are not entitled to draw salaries for their services.

The accounting conventions which cover partnerships reflect the above. Unlike a limited company where directors draw salaries, partners share in profits. So any money a partner draws is not a debit to the profit and loss account because it does not represent expenses of the business. Drawings are the use to which profits are put by the partners individually. This accounting convention is not helpful to a lender, who will not see a major distinction between drawings and other types of remuneration.

After all, the main aim of a partner in business is to generate an income for him or herself. For all practical purposes, this income is an 'expense' of the firm. The banker will be interested in the profit left over after drawings, as this will provide the prime source of repayment for borrowing.

In some partnerships there is very limited control over the amount that partners take out as drawings on a daily/weekly/monthly basis. It can often come as quite a shock to partners to find, when their accounts are drawn up, that they have anticipated profits to far too great an extent. Good financial control is as essential for a partnership as for any other business, but where partnerships are small and the individuals concerned more interested in their professional competence, the importance of good management information is sometimes neglected.

Case 1

Convey, Litigate and Probate are a firm of solicitors with eight partners operating from four offices in local towns. The partnership has expanded rapidly by acquisition of other firms in recent years to reach its present position. Its long-term aim is to expand its commercial client base and reduce reliance on conveyancing. No legal aid work is undertaken.

Two of the four offices bank with you, and you currently mark an overdraft limit of £250,000 for the firm. There have been occasional excesses over this limit, and the account is showing a hard core, which is on a rising trend. The other offices bank with two of your competitors. You currently have £1.4 million of clients' money on deposit.

In addition to the partnership itself, three of the partners bank with you in their personal capacity. You are aware that each of these has a minimum equity in his house of £150,000.

The senior partner calls to see you. He is going to take sole charge of the firm's finances, and as part of a process of tightening control he wishes to deal with only one bank. He asks if you will agree an increased overdraft limit of £500,000 in return for handling all the firm's banking.

In conversation you learn that the partnership is going to make strenuous efforts to increase fee income, and is seeking to recruit an extra partner for each office. Each new partner will be expected to provide £35,000 in capital.

This firm of solicitors is an important customer, which is having problems because of poor financial control. The substantial clients' account balances that are maintained will have to be an important factor in the assessment of the proposition as, if the lending is declined, they will almost certainly be lost to another bank. However, if the proposition is agreed, there is the prospect of gaining more valuable credit balances.

Analysis of the accounts shows that the net worth of the firm is declining steadily, mainly as a result of high partners' drawings. Gearing is worsening and cannot be calculated in June Year B because of the negative position shown. The partnership is currently being financed by creditors and banks – an unstable position.

Drawings have to be regarded as an expense of the business, and should be deducted to arrive at a 'true' net profit. On this basis, no profit has been made for the past two years, and the performance for the 12 months to June Year B is a loss of approximately £123,000. Overheads are rising much faster than income, and the partners' drawings over recent months have been unacceptably high. The only good sign is that the profit performance over the last six months was an improvement on the first half of the year.

There is, however, a long-term plan that seems sensible. Conveyancing is likely to be less profitable in the future, and the short-term aim of increasing fee income must be right, given the high overheads.

The proposed capital injection of £140,000 will improve both the balance sheet and the liquidity of the firm, but some formal projections ought to be seen, and it will be extremely important to judge whether the extra partners can produce more in fees than they will cost in overheads and drawings. It will also be an important factor to decide whether new partners will actually be prepared to commit capital to the firm in its current state.

There is no clearly defined source of repayment for the requested facility, and a decision based on future projections will still be an act of faith in the management of the firm, which to date has been less than perfect. There is therefore a strong case to be made for declining to take on the risk. However, I believe that most banks would be unwilling to sacrifice the valuable credit balances and the other contacts that the firm brings with it. There are further significant credit balances to be gained – a total of £3 million in the balance sheet.

It also needs to be recognized that with joint and several liability, the partners' personal assets stand behind the business. Three partners alone have equity in their houses of £450,000, so the bank is unlikely to be on risk unless they have other

CONVEY, LITIGATE & PROBATE: ALL OFFICES
BALANCE SHEETS

	30 June Year A £	31 Dec. Year A £	30 June Year B £
Fixed assets			
Short leasehold property	29,528	28,712	27,897
Equipment and fittings	83,466	97,111	130,745
Motor vehicles	37,740	55,271	72,208
	150,734	181,094	230,850
Current assets			
Work in progress	128,436	158,258	193,113
Debtors	289,290	267,036	352,159
Cash in hand, at bank and building society	5,299	64,498	56,603
Current liabilities	423,025	489,792	601,875
Bank overdraft	209,242	341,901	482,828
Bank loans	10,000	9,960	10,887
Creditors	208,016	223,486	274,020
	427,258	575,347	767,735
Net current liabilities	(4,233)	(85,555)	(165,860)
Creditors: due after more than one year			
Bank loan	20,846	18,613	15,013
Creditors	9,533	37,144	56,478
	30,379	55,757	71,491
	116,122	39,782	(6,501)
Clients' accounts			
Bank balances	1,484,253	1,686,808	3,090,416
Amounts owing to clients	(1,484,253)	(1,686,808)	(3,090,416)
Total net (liabilities)/assets	116,122	39,782	(6,501)
Partners' capital and current accounts			
Balance at start of period	132,756	116,122	39,782
Profit for period	201,260	40,114	95,858
Drawings	(217,894)	(116,454)	(142,141)
Balance at end of period	116,122	39,782	(6,501)

PROFIT AND LOSS ACCOUNT

	12 months ended 30 June Year A £	6 months ended 31 Dec. Year A £	12 monrhs ended 30 June Year B £
Fees receivable	1,125,439	681,327	1,518,532
Commission receivable	10,661	5,758	14,069
Bank interest receivable	68,167	49,864	100,809
Rent receivable	18,728	16,047	29,350
	1,222,995	752,996	1,662,760
Overheads			
Staff salaries and pensions	492,188	334,518	745,756
Other personnel costs	21,310	19,127	45,108
Motor and travelling	31,264	16,670	37,874
Entertaining	11,892	9,082	18,853
Rent and rates	83,473	57,795	110,230
Heat, light and power	7,272	4,179	10,895
Leasing and maintenance of office equipment	30,538	13,453	59,256
Repairs and renewals	8,111	15,322	43,071
Insurances	34,998	21,164	43,015
Printing, postage, advertising and stationery	59,621	42,150	94,115
Telephone	34,549	25,614	51,187
Subscriptions, donations, books and courses	14,843	10,062	26,455
Sundries	20,130	14,230	24,427
Professional indemnity claims	14,584	5,800	5,800
Professional charges	18,254	10,377	14,751
Accountancy fees	15,445	8,564	20,871
Provision for bad debts	23,174	50,101	48,624
Bank charges and interest	49,276	18,361	48,125
Depreciation	50,813	36,313	78,375
	1,021,735	712,882	1,526,788
Net profit for the year/period	201,260	40,114	135,972

RATIOS AND OTHER INFORMATION

	June Year A	Dec. Year A	June Year B
Current ratio	1:0.99	1:0.85	1:0.78
Acid test	1:0.69	1:0.57	1:0.68
Credit given (days)	93	72	85
Credit taken (days)	205	163	180
Net margin	17.9	5.9 (6 months)	9.0
Interest cover (times)	4.1	2.2 (6 months)	2.8
Net gearing (%)	202	769	

substantial liabilities about which it is not aware. It would obviously be prudent to tie in the partners' assets by taking second charges over their houses, but with a solicitors' firm of this nature these are unlikely to be on offer.

Some element of trust in the integrity of the partners will be necessary, at least in the short term. If, despite the firm's change of course, matters continue to deteriorate, then it would be appropriate to seek tangible security.

This is a very marginal proposition, but I suspect that most banks will agree – somewhat reluctantly – to provide the increased facilities. There would, however, have to be a suitable monitoring package, and it will be essential to have better financial management in place to provide this.

Case 2

Arthur Puff and Ian Hype are in their early 30s. They are partners in a firm of estate agents called Puff & Hype, which banks with one of your competitors.

Puff and Hype call to see you and tell you the following:

(a) They set up in business five years ago when they bought out an existing estate agency with one office. They have expanded, and now have four offices with plans to open more.

(b) Although last year was a difficult one for estate agents generally, because of the poor level of house sales in the area, Puff and Hype have been able to increase their market share through a high level of promotion and advertising effort.

(c) They currently enjoy an overdraft facility of £250,000 from their bank, secured by second mortgages on their houses, which have a joint equity valued at £400,000.

(d) They expect the house market to improve soon, and consider that they should build on their advertising and promotion expenditure by opening at least two more offices. They require their overdraft to be increased to £400,000.

(e) At the same time they wish to revise their security arrangements and have the charges on their houses released. In substitution, they offer a £400,000 guarantee from a property company called Puff & Hype Properties Ltd in which they are the only directors and shareholders. Puff & Hype Properties Ltd has net assets of £450,000 following a recent revaluation of its property assets.

(f)   Their present bank has refused both requests (in (d) and (e) above). Puff and Hype believe this is because the bank has its own estate agency subsidiary and does not wish to help a competitor business. They have approached you with the same request because your bank does not have any involvement in estate agency.

This situation involves two young estate agents who have done well to establish a business that is paying them a good income. Their excuse for wishing to transfer the business from another bank may be plausible, but there are a number of warning signs. The business has expanded rapidly, despite adverse conditions in the marketplace, and the partners are prepared to take higher risks to continue this process.

However, the financial structure of the business is unstable. After deducting goodwill, it appears that the business may never have had any tangible net worth. Gearing, in reality, is very high although, with no net worth, no ratio can be calculated. In fact the whole business is being financed by the creditors and the bank.

Profitability has been poor. The partners' drawings are an expense of the business, and need to be deducted before a 'true profit' can be struck. In fact, only in Year B was a true profit made. The performance in Year C was a loss of around £120,000. The partners have been paying themselves far too much, and also seem to have invested heavily in motor vehicles in recent months. A high cost base has been built up, which will not be easy to reverse should market conditions not improve.

The poor current ratio reflects the heavy dependence on creditors, and credit taken is uncomfortably high, even though it probably includes the partners' personal tax liabilities, which may not have to be met immediately. Although the figure has come down in Year C, it has been substituted by bank borrowing, and there is the suggestion that there may have been excesses, given that the Year C bank overdraft exceeded the limit. It would be vital for copies of past bank statements to be seen.

There are no detailed projections demonstrating the effects of the expansion plan, and some ought to be produced. In any event, as most of the expenditure is on fixed assets, any borrowing is likely to have a substantial hard core. It is very difficult in the short term to see how, even if the facility was granted by way of loan, this could be repaid.

A. PUFF AND I. HYPE (Trading as Puff & Hype Estate Agents)
BALANCE SHEET

As at 31 March	Year A		Year B		Year C	
	£	£	£	£	£	£
Fixed assets						
Short leasehold properties	609		3,387		67,115	
Furniture, fittings and office equipment	5,815		15,661		45,071	
Motor vehicles	32,531	38,955	37,634	56,682	106,322	218,508
Goodwill		40,000		40,000		40,000
Current assets						
Cash	250		8,393		408	
Debtors	44,937		79,355		106,624	
	45,187		87,748		107,032	
Current liabilities						
Creditors	141,028		150,792		186,464	
Bank overdraft	28,870		–		266,838	
	169,898		150,792		453,302	
Net current liabilities		(124,711)		(63,044)		(346,270)
		(45,756)		33,638		(87,762)
Represented by:						
Partners:						
Capital accounts						
Opening balance		(17,213)		(45,756)		3,638
Profit for the year		13,633		128,188		27,203
Drawings		(42,176)		(78,794)		(148,603)
Closing balance		(45,756)		3,638		(117,762)
Partners' loans		–		30,000		30,000
		(45,756)		33,638		(87,762)

RATIOS

	Year A	Year B	Year C
Current ratio	0.27:1	0.58:1	0.24:1
Credit given (days)	60	55	52
Credit taken (days)	370	285	164
Net gearing	–	–	–
Interest cover (before drawings) (times)	2.2	10.8	2.7
Profit as % of commissions	5.0	24.5	3.6

PROFIT AND LOSS ACCOUNT

As at 31 March	Year A £	Year A £	Year B £	Year B £	Year C £	Year C £
Commission receivable		273,161		523,959		759,062
Deposit interest		14		194		105
		273,175		524,153		759,167
Expenses						
Salaries and commissions	88,813		159,525		239,145	
Rent and rates	16,181		16,302		21,773	
Insurance	1,330		836		7,865	
Advertising	52,481		94,814		230,259	
Printing, postage and stationery	.	16,734	8,254	10,929		
Travelling and motor expenses		32,220	40,794	78,623		
Interest and bank charges	10,928		13,109		16,200	
Professional fees	5,152		5,246		22,204	
Light and heat	1,751		2,141		2,980	
Telephone	7,605		10,769		20,368	
Repairs and sundries	5,734		13,680		20,712	
Depreciation	20,613	259,542	30,495	395,965	60,906	731,964
Profit for the year		13,633		128,188		27,203

The present facility is probably just about adequately secured, even though it is by second charges on matrimonial homes. The proposed new security arrangements are a non-starter. It is very difficult to see where there could be any benefit for Puff & Hype Properties Ltd, and its interest needs to be separated from that of its directors. The proposed arrangement would be contrary to the provisions of Section 330 of the Companies Act 1985.

There is plenty of evidence here of poor financial control, and Puff & Hype's present bankers are right to be cautious. The risks involved in the business, and the management philosophy of Messrs Puff & Hype, suggest that this is not an account to be taken on.

Case 3

Harry Wisdom has maintained an account at your branch since he started his course at the dental school of the local university 10 years ago. Since he graduated five years ago he has worked as a full-time associate for a practice in the area, and is currently earning around £18,000 per annum.

Mr Wisdom has requested a meeting with you today. You are advised that the balances on his accounts are as follows:

Current account £500 Cr

Deposit account £1,500

Loan £900, repayable at £100 per month.

At the meeting Mr Wisdom explains that Colin Gate, the principal of another local practice, was killed in an accident while on holiday in June. The practice was operated by Mr Gate and two part-time lady associates, who were paid 45% of their gross fees, an arrangement similar to Mr Wisdom's contract with his own principals. For the past three months the lady associates have continued to operate Mr Gate's practice, but apparently they wish to return to the original arrangement as soon as possible.

Mr Gate's practice has used the ground floor of his home, which was valued last week for Mr Wisdom by a local estate agent at £53,000. Mr Wisdom has been negotiating with Mrs Gate to purchase the practice. They have agreed on the following basis:

House	£50,000
Equipment	£15,000
Goodwill	£15,000

Mr Wisdom has examined the equipment: it is in good order, and in his opinion is worth over £20,000.

COLIN GATE, DENTAL PRACTITIONER
INCOME AND EXPENDITURE ACCOUNT

As at 31 March	Year A		Year B		Year C	
	£	£	£	£	£	£
Fees		66,700		71,800		76,300
Materials/drugs, lab fees, etc.	7,200		7,900		8,500	
Salaries – Associates	14,200		15,100		16,400	
– Staff	10,100		11,200		12,400	
Premises expenses	7,400		7,900		8,800	
Motor/travel expenses	1,800		1,900		2,100	
Sundries	1,500		1,800		1,900	
Finance costs	2,000		1,800		2,100	
Depreciation	5,600		4,800		4,600	
Total expenses		49,800		52,400		56,800
Net income		16,900		19,400		19,500

BALANCE SHEET

	Year A		Year B		Year C	
Fixed assets						
Equipment		20,400		18,600		17,500
Motor vehicles		6,000		4,500		8,500
		26,400		23,100		26,000
Debtors	6,1 00		11,300		6,900	
Stock/work in progress	700		900		900	
	6,800		12,200		7,800	
Creditors	2,100		2,400		2,800	
Bank	6,100		6,800		2,300	
Hire purchase	4,000		2,200		4,000	
Loan (father)	10,000		10,000		10,000	
	22,200		21,400		19,100	
Net current liabilities		(15,400)		(9,200)		(11,300)
Net tangible assets		11,000		13,900		14,700
Financed by:						
Capital b/fwd		9,600		11,000		13,900
Net income	16,900		19,400		19,500	
Less drawings	(15,500)	1,400	(16,500)	2,900	(18,700)	800
Capital c/fwd		11,000		13,900		14,700

RATIOS AND OTHER INFORMATION

	Year A	Year B	Year C
Current ratio	0.31:1	0.57:1	0.41:1
Acid test	0.27:1	0.52:1	0.36:1
Gearing (%)	183	137	111
Interest cover (times)	9.5	11.8	10.3
Credit given (days)	33	57	33
Credit taken (days)	106	111	120
Net margin (before drawings) (%)	25.3	27.0	25.6

He is keen to purchase Mr Gate's practice. It is situated only two miles from his present surgery, and he expects some of his existing patients to follow him, with the result that the income of the practice should increase by at least £10,000 over a year.

Mr Wisdom explains that he bought his house five years ago with the help of a building society endowment mortgage of £25,000. The house was valued last week at £45,000, and the estate agent confirmed that there is a good demand for this type of property. He has some cash – £6,000 – saved in a building society account, but there is a tax demand of nearly £3,000 due on 1 January.

Mrs Gate has let him have her late husband's accounts, which he hands to you. Mr Wisdom asks if your bank can assist him with the purchase of Mr Gate's practice.

This proposition concerns the purchase of a professional practice for a dentist. Mr Wisdom is a longstanding good customer. There is background evidence of an ability to save in the balances of his accounts, with both the bank and the building society. However, he has never run a business before, and although it is natural that he should wish to have his own practice, the proposition needs to be approached with caution. Given Wisdom's lack of business experience, ideally he should use an accountant to produce a business plan for both himself and the bank.

Acquiring a partnership is not like acquiring a limited company where by buying shares all the assets and liabilities in the balance sheet are purchased. Mr Wisdom is going to acquire only the equipment and premises (the house) of the business, together with a payment to reflect the value of the future income stream of the business – the goodwill. The proposition falls into two parts:

(a)   the house purchase;

(b)   the purchase of the practice.

Taking the house purchase first, the figures are:

	£	£
Purchase price		50,000
Sale of existing house	45,000	
Less mortgage	25,000	20,000
Requirement		30,000 plus expenses

In isolation, there should be no problem in agreeing a mortgage of £30,000 or even £35,000 for Wisdom, given his current and potential income. There may of course be a need for a bridging loan, and pressure may come from Mrs Gate for this to be open-ended. In all the circumstances, it would probably be unwise for Wisdom to enter into an open-ended bridging loan as, if there were any difficulty in selling his own house, he would be starting up in business on his own with additional interest pressures, which he will not need when trying to find his feet in the new venture. A bridging loan on a closed basis should not, however, pose any problem.

Turning to the purchase of the practice, the amount required is:

	£
Equipment	15,000
Goodwill	5,000
	30,000

Is the asking price reasonable? Wisdom ought to be reasonably competent in assessing the value of the equipment, but if there is any doubt, an independent outside valuation should probably be undertaken. The value of the goodwill is more problematical. Essentially, this is what the business is worth to a purchaser because it assures him/her of a future income. The figures show that the business has been steadily profitable, and at £15,000 the goodwill payment is less than one year's profit before drawings. On this basis, it looks reasonable.

Wisdom has cash available around £5,000 towards the purchase, but some of this may be needed to meet legal expenses and so on. Moreover, there will be a need for a working capital facility. On the Year C balance sheet, debtors and stock amounted to £7,800 while creditors were able to finance only £2,800 of this. It would appear that there is a need for a working capital overdraft facility of around £5,000 to cover the gap, perhaps even more. This is where a business plan would be useful and, in particular, a detailed cash flow forecast. In any event, a budget is going to be needed to establish on reasonable assumptions that Wisdom can afford the repayments on a loan of say £25,000, plus his mortgage.

Repayments at an interest rate of say 13% for a loan of £25,000 over 10 years, would amount to nearly £5,000 per annum. The accounts for the practice show finance and depreciation costs in Year C at £6,700, which would be available to meet repayments, and there is the possibility of a higher net income if Wisdom can indeed bring the £10,000 per annum of business with him from his present surgery. Overall, the figures would suggest that repayment should be viable.

The total borrowing should amount to:

	£
Mortgage, say	35,000
Loan	25,000
Overdraft, say	5,000
	65,000

As security, there would be the house worth £50,000, so there would be a considerable shortfall. It would obviously be important to have professional valuations on Wisdom's current property and the new house. The shortfall in security need not be of undue concern, provided repayment viability can be firmly established. It would be unrealistic to take chattel mortgages over the equipment, but if things did not work out, the practice could probably be sold for the sort of amount that would reduce any residual indebtedness. It would of course be vital to have full life cover over Wisdom's life for all the borrowing.

Retailers

8

Most bank branches have a number of small retailers on their books, and it is probably fair to say that this type of business provides more than its fair share of heartache to lenders. Retailing is quite an easy business to get into, with the result that many people who start up do so with very little experience of running a business and little true appreciation of the difficulties involved.

The power of the large supermarket and other substantial retail groups in the United Kingdom has made many types of small retailer an endangered species. For example, on current estimates it is thought that the three largest supermarket chains in the United Kingdom have in excess of 43% of the grocery trade. The buying power this gives them makes it virtually impossible for smaller businesses to compete on price; and the whole concept of 'one stop' shopping militates against the small retailer. The disappearance of some types of small retailer from the High Street, such as the family butcher, is a reflection of this. In the future in the United Kingdom small retailers will probably have to specialize in some way to be successful. To win in the marketplace they will have to offer something extra in terms of convenience (for example, location and opening hours), quality, special types of goods, service and so on. In technical marketing terms, they will have to become niche players.

When looking at new propositions for small retailers the extent to which they can be seen to fill a potential niche in the market is an interesting test, which may give useful pointers to their capacity to succeed. In recent years certain ethnic groups have proved themselves as successful small retailers in businesses where long opening hours with the commensurate requirement that the proprietors must be prepared to work particularly hard, such as newsagents, chemists and small grocery shops, have been an important feature.

Quality of management

On the face of it, a shop is a very simple business to run. Goods are bought at one price, held in stock, and sold at a higher price to make a profit. There are none of the worries that exist in relation to more complex businesses, such as manufacturing, with the need to train a skilled workforce, maintain plant and machinery, meet production deadlines and so on. For this reason, retailing attracts more than its fair share of 'amateur' businessmen. Many people are attracted to the thought of being self-employed, and do not fully appreciate the difficulties involved. The thought of running a small restaurant or some sort of fashion clothes shop represents a long-held dream for some people. However, both the restaurant and fashion clothes businesses are highly competitive, so success is not easy to come by, and the failure rate is high.

Where existing businesses are concerned, the lender will at least have a track record of performance as a means of assessing quality of management. More problematical will be instances where a new business is being acquired or established by someone who has not been a retailer before. In practice it is virtually impossible to know whether someone will or will not be successful. It is obviously helpful if someone has either had experience of the type of trade or has had responsibility for running some business activity before.

Anyone who is going to run his or her own business needs a high degree of enthusiasm, but it is possible to let enthusiasm turn into over-optimism. It is extremely difficult to forecast sales where small retailers are concerned. Some people try to carry out market surveys, but these are of very dubious value. It would be appropriate for some sort of business plan to be produced, and often the assistance of an outside accountant will be enlisted. In such instances, it is often the case that forecasts are produced 'from the bottom line up', so that sales receipts are shown at the level necessary to produce the required result in terms of cash flow produced to repay a given level of borrowing. It needs to be understood that the motivation behind documents produced by outside accountants is usually to maximize their clients' chances of obtaining a loan, and a lender must concentrate on distinguishing between the story being told in the business plan and the underlying soundness of the proposition.

In the majority of cases the lender will not have a great deal to go on to form a sound judgement of the proposition. Where an existing business is being purchased, there will be some track record reflected in audited accounts, but very often there will be an explanation that these have been produced 'for the tax man' and so do not reflect the true performance of the business. I shall return to this point below. Where the lender cannot assess the soundness of the proposition with sufficient certainty, the only case in which it should be agreed is if there is strong security cover. Again, this is a point that I shall return to below.

Financial statements

More than for any other type of business, the accounts of small retailers are susceptible to being produced for 'tax purposes'. Lenders are regularly told that the true performance of such businesses is in fact much better than that shown in the accounts. There is an argument for treating such accounts as being an accurate representation of the business's performance, but the practice of producing accounts 'for the tax man' is so widespread that this approach is not helpful. The important thing that a lender wishes to establish is the true financial position of the business and its real cash-generating capacity.

The reason why small retailers are able to 'adjust' their accounts for tax purposes is that theirs is mainly a cash business. It is relatively easy, therefore, to take cash out of the till so that it never appears as sales income or reaches the bottom line in the accounts as profit. Another means of reducing profit for tax purposes by certain retailers is to take goods for 'own consumption'. For example, the owner of a grocery store can simply take goods off the shelves that he or she would otherwise have to buy from income.

If cash is being taken out of the business without appearing in the books, it is not unreasonable to seek evidence as to where it has gone. Such cash must represent surplus income over and above the amount that the proprietor needs to maintain a reasonable lifestyle. In a small business a reasonable level of income for the proprietor is one of the costs that must always be borne if it is to have a stable future. Cash taken out of a business that forms part of the proprietor's normal income cannot be regarded as a hidden profit available to repay borrowing, unless it has been saved in some way or spent on 'luxuries'. Evidence of such a saving or expenditure may be available.

A lender should not expect to see a business that is supposedly generating more cash and profit than is passing through the books to be working close to its overdraft limit. So an examination of past bank statements showing the run of the bank account can be an informative exercise when trying to decide whether indeed a business's performance is really a lot better than it appears from its financial statements.

Most small retail businesses are run either as sole traders or as partnerships. This means that the income that the proprietor or proprietors take from the business is shown as 'drawings'. The accounting convention is that a profit for the business is added to the capital and any income withdrawn is taken from capital rather than out of profits. This is not helpful from a lender's point of view, as the proprietor's income is really a cost of the business and needs to be taken into account before the cash-generating capacity of the business is established. For most lenders, therefore, the 'true profit of a business' will be the net profit less the proprietor's drawings.

Security

With the large degree of uncertainty surrounding the viability of business plans for small retailers, adequate security is usually a key issue in the assessment. However, in many instances the only security available may be the business itself. The main asset of the retailing business will almost certainly be the premises, which will have a significant value if they are a freehold or long leasehold. But, in many instances, retail premises are held on occupational leases. An occupational lease is generally defined as a tenancy agreement, usually with a term of less than 30 years. The occupation of property is obtained in consideration of a rent payment, which is subject to regular reviews, usually at three to five or seven-year intervals.

While an occupational lease may have a good open-market value, it does not represent good security because only rarely will it have a forced sale value. This is because an occupational lease is likely to contain a bankruptcy clause whereby it will be forfeit if the lessee goes bankrupt or into liquidation – the precise occasion when a lender will be looking to sell the security. The lease will also be forfeit if rent is not paid, and it is not usually worthwhile for a lender to fund rent payments in order merely to retain the security. This is because any profit rental that would accrue between rent reviews will be eliminated at the next review. The consequence of this is that the value of the lease will usually be low compared with the annual rental payments. So it would not normally be sensible to meet, say, one or two quarters' rent to preserve the security unless there were very positive reasons for believing an early sale of the lease could be achieved.

The most prudent view to take of occupational leases is to regard them as having no security value at all. However, a lender with a charge over such a lease does have control over what is usually the major asset of a retailer. This means that the business cannot be disposed of without the borrowing being repaid, and for this reason alone it is usually advisable for a lender to take a charge on an occupational lease even though the forced-sale security value will be nil.

The security cover must have a sufficient margin to repay the borrowing in the event of the failure of the business. The appropriate size of security margin is an issue that is dealt with in *Bankers' Lending Techniques* in Chapter 8, 'Corporate lending and security'. Once an appropriate security margin has been decided upon, a lender must not allow this to be eroded. It is therefore appropriate, where most small retailers are concerned, for the vast bulk of the borrowing to be by way of loan, with overdrafts being kept to the absolute minimum.

As the success of any small retailer will depend crucially upon the proprietor, a suitable amount of life cover will be required, and health insurance may also be appropriate.

Case 1

Your customer, Mr Peach, is 52 years old and has banked with you for over 10 years. For the past five years he has been working as a salesman for a local motor components company. The company has recently gone into liquidation, and he has been made redundant.

Peach calls to see you. At his age, he thinks it is unlikely that he will be able to get another job as a salesman. He has seen an advertisement in the local newspaper offering for sale a greengrocery business in a nearby small town. The asking price is £30,000 for the lease, fixtures and fittings and goodwill. He has visited the shop and obtained copies of the last three years' accounts for the business from the present owner, Mr Grapes.

Mr Peach has decided to buy the business and is willing to offer the asking price. In conversation the following facts emerge:

(a)   Peach has £7,000 of redundancy money to put towards the purchase, and wants a 10-year loan of £23,000 to meet the balance.

(b)   His wife, aged 50, who has had past experience of book-keeping, will be willing to help him in the shop, and he does not expect to employ anyone else.

(c)   The lease of the shop was originally granted for 21 years with reviews every seven years. It has 15 years to run. The current rent is £1,300 per annum, and Peach's enquiries of local estate agents suggest that this is cheap, with typical rents for similar shops in the area now being £3,000 per annum.

(d)   Peach and his wife own their house, which he believes is worth £60,000, with a mortgage of £2,000 outstanding.

(e)   Peach used to have a company car with his job, but lost this when he was made redundant. He has since paid £2,000 cash for a small secondhand car, which he will use to get to and from the shop.

(f)   Grapes has told Peach that the accounts for the business have been 'produced for tax purposes' and that he has been regularly taking £200 per week 'out of the till' in cash. Grapes has told Peach that he is selling the business in order to emigrate to Australia.

This proposition represents a fairly straightforward shop-purchase situation that, in company with many such proposals, is not particularly easy to deal with. It involves someone who has been made redundant, is looking for a new occupation, and sees running a shop as being an appropriate way out. Mr Peach is a longstanding customer, and his bank would wish to try to help him. He has a background in selling and his wife has book-keeping skills, both of which may be helpful in running a business. However, neither Mr nor Mrs Peach is particularly young to be taking on what will be quite a physically demanding job, and they will be 'amateurs' at the trade.

The proposition is being presented in quite a naïve way. Peach seems to be requesting only the exact amount of the purchase consideration. Will this be enough? What about legal expenses and so on? Grapes appears to have needed a van to run the business – presumably for wholesale purchases/deliveries – and a similar form of transport will probably be needed, although Peach's present car could probably be traded in. There may also be a need for working capital although, looking at the recent balance sheets, the creditor figure more than covers current asset needs. The question has to be asked, however, whether the same amount of credit that has been available to Grapes will still be available to Peach.

The asking price of £30,000 looks high. A rent review is imminent, so the lease itself will have relatively little value. With profits in Year C of nearly £9,000, Peach would be paying more than three times annual profits, and this could probably only be justified on the back of the 'hidden profit' of £200 a week.

S. GRAPES
(Trading as Grapes Greengrocers)
BALANCE SHEETS

As at 30 September	Year A £	Year A £	Year B £	Year B £	Year C £	Year C £
Current assets						
Cash and bank	305		264		320	
Debtors and prepayments	91		103		223	
Stock	300	696	300	667	350	893
Current liabilities						
Creditors	2,066		2,294		3,114	
Bank loan	3,455	5,521	4,666	6,960	3,716	6,830
Net current assets		(4,825)		(6,293)		(5,937)
Fixed assets						
Lease	5,000		5,000		5,000	
Van	560		2,400		1,920	
Fixtures and fittings	670	6,230	648	8,048	818	7,738
Net assets		1,405		1,755		1,801
Represented by:						
Capital account						
Opening balance		(847)		1,405		1,755
Add: Net profit for the year		8,236		5,431		7,024
		7,389		6,836		8,779
Less: Drawings		5,984		5,081		6,978
		1,405		1,755		1,801

TRADING AND PROFIT AND LOSS ACCOUNT

12 months ended 30 September	Year A £	Year A £	Year B £	Year B £	Year C £	Year C £
Sales		56,745		52,046		57,448
Less: Cost of sales						
Opening stock	300		300		300	
Purchases	43,198		38,523		42,461	
	43,498		38,823		42,761	
Less: Closing stock	300	43,198	300	38,523	350	42,411
Gross profit		13,547		13,523		15,037
Less: Expenses						
Rent	1,300		1,300		1,300	
Rates and water rates	573		607		659	
Light, heat and power	193		207		224	
Paper	306		334		312	
Vehicle expenses	792		1,303		966	
Printing and stationery	111		62		56	
Repairs and renewals	4		952		61	
Insurance	35		35		35	
Telephone	140		190		180	
Wages	444		1,219		2,472	
Bank charges	856		961		977	
Accountancy fees	170		190		200	
Bad debts	56		–		–	
Depreciation	216		672		571	
Loss on sale of car	115	5,311	60	8,092	–	8,013
Net profit		8,236		5,431		7,024

RATIOS AND OTHER INFORMATION

	Year A	Year B	Year C
Gross profit margin (%)	24	26	26
Net profit margin (%)	15	10	12
Credit taken (days)	17	22	27

Peach will be putting in a stake of £7,000 himself, and although many textbooks talk about a proprietor needing to put in 0% of any requirement, in my opinion this is not very realistic. On the basis that Peach intends to be a sole trader, there will be unlimited liability and his personal assets will be on the line, particularly the equity in his house. All things considered, £7,000 probably represents a reasonable proprietor's stake.

The viability of repayment will obviously be the key issue in deciding whether to agree the proposition. Assuming an interest rate of say 13%, £23,000 repayable over 10 years would require annual repayments of approximately £4,100. The sales performance of the business has not been steady and needs to be investigated but, provided the Year C figure is not exceptional and can be repeated, the sort of cash income available to meet repayments can be computed as follows:

	£
Profit	7,025
Add back: Depreciation	571
Wages	2,472
Bank charges	976
	11,044
But rent will rise next year – deduct	1,700
Sustainable cash flow	9,344

This will leave the Peaches roughly £5,200 per annum to live on, which looks rather tight. So the key issue will be the extra cash income that Grapes has said he has been taking 'out of the till'. As has been mentioned before, there is little doubt that sole traders in this kind of business do take money 'out of the till' to avoid tax. Some cash will have been taken out, and the question is: how much?

Peach needs to find some proof of the cash income, and this might be discovered as follows:

(a) Grape's bank statements, which, while not showing the cash taken out of the till, will give an indication of how tight cash has been overall.

(b) By spending some time working in the shop alongside Grapes and checking the actual takings.

(c)　There is some evidence in the accounts that there may have been more cash around. The maintenance of the overall gross profit figure, despite a reduction in sales in Year B and the subsequent holding of the gross profit margin at 26% on increased sales in Year C, may be an indication that the true gross profit is actually higher than indicated in the bald figures.

However, in the end no lender can be sure that this business is able to generate sufficient cash to repay the borrowing, so any facility granted will have to be fully secured.

The lease of the shop will probably have no value as security but should be charged to give the bank control of the major asset of the business. The main security would have to be a second charge over the Peaches' house, which looks as though it has equity of £58,000. There will be a need for life cover, but health insurance – while it would be ideal – would probably have a prohibitive cost, given Peach's age.

It is a very marginal proposition. There is adequate security cover, but Peach's lack of experience and difficulty in verifying the capacity of the business to repay count against it. However, given the extent of the security cover, in most instances this is a proposition that would be agreed. The bottom line is that even if Peach fails to run the business satisfactorily, it would probably be sold for something, and the equity in the house should ensure that the lender gets out.

Case 2

Mike's Bikes is a family-run cycle shop, which has been established for over 50 years near a large city centre. It sells and repairs cycles, and stocks and sells cycle accessories. The business currently has an exclusive franchise arrangement with a major British manufacturer and sells only its cycles. For this, a 10% discount off normal trade prices is given.

Recently, a new out-of-town shopping centre has been built, and this contains a multiple retailer that sells cycles. The proprietor of Mike's Bikes has decided to retire and sell the business.

Two of your customers, James Alexander, aged 39, and Philip Dunn, aged 28, who are cycle enthusiasts, wish to buy the business. Alexander is currently a sales manager with a cycle firm and Dunn is a fireman. They have offered to purchase the stock and goodwill of the business as follows:

Goodwill	£20,000
Stock at valuation	£25,000 (estimate)
	£45,000

They tell you:

(a) The goodwill includes the Mike's Bikes trade name, and will be purchased in two instalments in Year D and Year E.

(b) The current proprietor owns the freehold of the shop, which he intends to retain. They hope to negotiate a 10-year lease at a rent of £12,000 p.a.

(c) They intend to dispense with the current exclusive franchise arrangement and move the shop up market by stocking higher-priced foreign cycles as well.

(d) They will be establishing a new limited company to acquire the stock and goodwill of Mike's Bikes.

(e) Alexander has £10,000 to put into the business, and owns a house with an equity of £2S,000. Dunn has no significant personal assets but his father would be prepared to provide a £10,000 guarantee.

(f) They have seen recent profit and loss figures and produced their own profit projection and cash flow forecast for their first year's trading. Based on their calculations, they need from the bank:

Overdraft	£10,000
Loan (7 years)	£16,000
	£26,000

This is another shop purchase proposition. Mike's Bikes is a well-established business, with a good profitable track record. Indeed, given the level of past profits, the price being paid for the goodwill looks very reasonable indeed. However, this may reflect the new competition in the marketplace, which could hit sales considerably.

The decision to dispense with the current franchise arrangement and to move up market is undoubtedly a risk, but this is probably necessary as it will be difficult to compete on price with the new multiple retailer. However, there is little evidence that there is a sufficient market for more expensive bikes in the area and some ought to be produced.

The management are something of an unknown quantity. Alexander ought to know the cycle business and should know something about selling. However, Dunn brings little but his enthusiasm with him. Neither of them appears to have had any experience of running their own business before.

The amount being requested is derived from the cash flow forecast and is the minimum needed. An examination of the forecast shows that the overdraft does not peak until the second goodwill payment is due, so it would be very important to monitor actual performance against budget to ensure that sufficient cash is generated for the second payment to be met. The projected profit and loss figures and cash flow forecast need to be examined rigorously and the underlying assumptions tested. For example, what evidence is there that the sales figure can be achieved, given the switch in the markets being attacked? The projected gross margin at 35% looks ambitious, particularly given the loss of the 10% discount that benefited the past figures.

The bottom-line profit needs to be adjusted to take account of the £12,000 per annum rent, which has not previously been charged, and interest, which is likely to amount to around £2,500 per annum. The overheads look realistic on the assumption that wages will be less with two proprietors willing to take less in remuneration than the previous one. Overall, net profit is likely to be around £12,000 and the net margin approximately 6%.

It will be important to establish that the credit-taken assumptions in the cash flow forecast are realistic. Otherwise, it could be the case that a significantly higher borrowing requirement will be needed. Will the suppliers of the higher-priced foreign bicycles be willing to give generous credit terms to a newly established business?

The initial capital stake in the business will in fact be negative, as the £10,000 Alexander has to put into the business will be more than wiped out by the goodwill payment of £20,000, leaving negative net assets at £10,000. Against this background, good security cover will be necessary. The business is to be established as a limited company, so a debenture can be taken, but it will have limited value in a business like this. The main asset will be stock, which is very 'mobile' and might easily disappear in the event of a liquidation. In fact, a debenture on this business is probably not worth taking.

MIKE'S BIKES
TRADING AND PROFIT AND LOSS ACCOUNT

12 months to 31 December	Year A	Year B	Year C	Projected next 12 months
	£	£	£	£
Sales	187,042	190,384	196,533	208,700
Cost of sales	125,668	124,248	128,779	135,655
Gross profit	61,374	66,136	67,754	73,045
Expenses				
Wages and National Insurance	18,579	18,711	16,372	10,000
Rates and water	3,247	3,178	3,477	3,178
Insurance	472	550	699	650
Heating and lighting	772	1,174	1,469	1,550
Telephone	331	370	336	400
Postage and carriage	116	120	110	140
Printing, stationery and wrapping	187	387	200	400
Advertising	779	339	772	500
Travelling and delivery	425	108	–	200
Audit and accountancy	454	480	520	500
Miscellaneous expenses	244	287	255	300
Staff refreshments	226	190	177	200
Repairs and renewals	(42)	285	303	200
Credit card charges	1,374	1,627	1,708	2,000
Depreciation	123	255	230	230
	27,287	28,061	26,628	20,448
Operating profit	34,087	38,075	41,126	52,597
Investment income received	4,367	4,575	1,592	–
	38,454	42,650	42,718	52,597
Director's remuneration	24,213	26,224	27,783	26,000
Profit before tax, interest and rent	14,241	16,426	14,935	26,597

RATIOS

Gross margin (%)	32.8	34.7	34.5	35.0
Net margin (%)	7.6	8.6	7.6	–

CASH FLOW FORECAST

	Year D April Budget £	May Budget £	June Budget £	July Budget £	Aug. Budget £
Receipts					
Sales (inc VAT) – Cash	17,188	21,068	18,136	22,498	21,601
Sales less VAT	14,946	18,320	15,770	19,563	18,787
Other trading income					
Loans received	16,000				
Capital introduced	10,000				
Disposal of assets					
Other receipts					
Total receipts	43,188	21,068	18,136	22,498	21,601
Payments					
Cash purchases	35,000				
Payments to creditors	4,500	14,172	15,694	11,787	14,623
Directors' remuneration	2,167	2,167	2,167	2,167	2,167
Wages/salaries/N.I.	834	834	834	834	834
Insurance	–	–	–	–	–
Transport/packaging	15	15	15	15	15
Rates	300	300	300	300	300
Services: Phone/heat/light	–	–	–	487	
Loan repayments	277	277	277	277	277
HP/leasing alarm system	112	–	–	–	–
Interest	–	–		143	–
Bank finance charges	85	85	85	85	85
Professional fees	–	–	–	–	–
Advertising	80	80	80	80	80
Rent	2,000	1,000	1,000	1,000	1,000
Miscellaneous	125	125	125	125	125
Access/Visa Charges	170	170	170	170	170
VAT	–	–	–	2574	–
Total payments	45,665	19,225	20,747	20,044	19,676
Opening bank balance	(1,700)	(4,177)	(2,334)	(4,945)	(2,491)
Closing bank balances	(4,177)	(2,334)	(4,945)	(2,491)	(566)

NOTES 1. Cash purchases for stock April Year D includes goodwill first payment (£10,000). Stock at valuation taken to be £25,000.

2. Opening bank balance from costs prior to trading: insurance £650; credit registration £150; Access/Visa registration £100; loan arrangement £500; solicitors' fees £300.

3. Cash purchase April Year E £10,000 second goodwill payment.

CASHFLOW FORECAST continued

| | | | | Year E | | | |
Sept. Budget £	Oct. Budget £	Nov. Budget £	Dec. Budget £	Jan. Budget £	Feb. Budget £	March Budget £	April Budget £
18,276	19,882	23,122	32,193	12,521	12,504	21,030	18,000
15,892	17,288	20,106	27,993	10,887	10,873	18,286	15,650
18,276	19,882	23,122	32,193	12,521	12,504	21,030	18,000
						10,000	
14,040	11,878	12,923	15,029	20,924	8,137	8,127	13,669
2,167	2,167	2,167	2,167	2,167	2,167	2,167	2,167
834	834	834	834	834	834	834	834
-	-	-	-	-	-	650	
15	15	15	15	15	15	15	15
300	300	300	300	300	300	300	300
-	487	-	-	487	-	-	487
277	277	277	277	277	277	277	277
-	-	-	150	-	-	-	-
-	62	-	-	24	-	-	49
85	85	85	85	85	85	85	85
							500
80	80	80	80	80	80	80	80
1,000	1,000	1,000	1,000	1,000	1,000	1,000	1,000
125	125	125	125	125	125	125	125
170	170	170	170	170	170	170	170
-	2,347	-	-	3,432	-	-	2,102
19,093	20,327	17,976	20,232	29,920	13,190	14,330	31,360
(566)	(1,383)	(1,828)	3,318	15,279	(2,120)	(2,806)	1,894
(1,383)	(1,828)	3,318	15,279	(2,120)	(2,806)	3,094	(9,466)

A charge should be taken on the lease, although this will have little security value. Guarantees from Alexander and Dunn will be necessary, and Alexander's guarantee ought to be supported by a second charge on his house, although the equity is relatively small. The guarantee from Dunn's father may have a value, but we know nothing about the father's assets, and given the high risks involved in this proposition, the guarantee would have to be supported. Life and health cover on both Alexander and Dunn would be appropriate.

This is a very marginal proposition, and backing enthusiasts in this kind of business can be very risky. It is virtually impossible to say whether the projections can be achieved, and the security on offer is weak. If the business starts very slowly, the deferred payment of £10,000 will loom very large. In fact the deferred payment is another form of borrowing, which will have to be repaid before the bank. On balance, the proposition is too risky and should be turned down.

Case 3

Ken and Mary Wagstaff have maintained a satisfactory joint account at your branch for a number of years. Mr Wagstaff is 41 years old and has been a manager of a newsagent's shop in your local shopping centre for five years.

Mr Wagstaff calls to see you. The company he works for is a national chain.

It has decided to dispose of a number of its shops, and he has the opportunity to buy the unit he manages. He tells you the following:

(a)   He believes that he will have to offer £67,000 to purchase the business.

(b)   The shop is leasehold. A 20-year lease was granted three and a half years ago at a rent of £10,000 per annum, subject to five-yearly reviews. The landlord is a national insurance company.

(c)   He has arrived at the purchase price as follows:

> Fixtures and fittings   £15,000
>
> Goodwill   £52,000

> Stock will be acquired at an agreed valuation. The current stock is worth around £30,000.

(d)   He has extracted the financial information set out below from the accounts, he submits to head office.

(e)   Mr and Mrs Wagstaff have £30,000 invested in building society accounts, which they inherited from Mrs Wagstaff's mother, who died last year.

(f)   The Wagstaffs jointly own their house, which they believe is worth £75,000 (subject to a £30,000 endowment mortgage). They also own a two-year-old van.

(g)   Mr Wagstaff's current salary from the shop is £18,000 per annum. His wife, who has not worked recently, would assist him in the shop, and this will enable him to save wages of £8,000 currently paid to other staff.

Wagstaff asks for your assistance to purchase the business.

The Wagstaffs have been good customers of the bank and can provide a substantial capital stake from their own resources. Mr Wagstaff has a good knowledge of the business, having run it for five years. Under his stewardship it has apparently been successful. All the indications therefore are that the management will be good, but it is still necessary to question why the national chain has decided to sell and what the competition is and how it might develop. For example, newsagents are facing increasing competition from supermarkets.

PROFIT AND LOSS SUMMARY

| | Actuals 12 months ending | | | Budget 3 mths to: 12 mths to: | |
	30 June Year A	30 June Year B	30 June Year C	30 Sep. Year C	30 Sep. Year D
Sales	415,000	450,000	487,000	133,000	584,000
Gross profit	73,500	82,500	92,100	24,000	110,000
Gross profit (%)	17.7%	18.3%	18.9%	18.0%	18.8%
Salaries (inc. manager)	31,700	34,400	37,100	9,500	38,000
Rent	10,000	10,000	10,000	2,500	16,000
Other expenses	15,300	17,100	18,300	4,700	20,000
Net profit	16,500	21,000	26,700	7,300	36,000
Net profit (%)	4.0%	4.7%	5.5%	5.5%	6.2%
Credit taken (days)	36	41	35	42	35
Stock turnover (days)	22	20	21	25	21

The price being paid will be particularly important. No value is being put on the lease, which is probably sensible, but a view needs to be taken as to whether the fixtures and fittings are in good condition and are indeed worth £15,000. A bigger issue is the value of the goodwill. At just under two times last year's profit, it does not look unreasonable. An alternative method of assessment would be to look at goodwill in relation to turnover. At five and a half weeks' sales, the value of goodwill again does not seem unreasonable.

The amount Wagstaff needs to borrow is ostensibly £67,000 less the £30,000 he and his wife have in the building society, i.e. £37,000. Legal expenses etc. need to be added and, more importantly, a view has to be taken of what size of working capital facility is required to finance ongoing trading. £30,000, or thereabouts, will have to be paid for the stock immediately – although some of this should be capable of being financed on credit as replacement items are bought. An analysis of the historical credit taken and stock turnover figures indicates that, long term, it may be possible to finance virtually all the stock on credit. However, it must be recognized that the current credit terms are for a national chain, and may not be available for a small shop. This issue has to be pursued with Wagstaff and a simple cash flow forecast drawn up in the light of whatever credit terms he can obtain. However, it does look as though an overdraft limit of £10,000/£15,000 ought to be enough.

A term loan of say £40,000 over five to ten years should be well within the capacity of the business to repay given its strong track record of profitability. Repayments over five years will be around £10,000 against last year's net profit of £26,700. Some caution is needed because both the historical and budgeted net profit are for the current owners, and may not reflect the new situation. Also, the rent is due to jump by £12,000 in a full year according to the budget. On the other hand, wage costs should reduce by £8,000 per annum. Wagstaff needs to produce a proper new budget.

A charge over the lease is required as security, and a second charge over the matrimonial home will also be appropriate.

Overall the request looks straightforward and is capable of agreement, subject to a satisfactory new budget and cash flow forecast.

Case 4

· ·

Felix Spooner, aged 52, is a dealer in antiques. He runs his business through a limited company called Felix Spooner (Antiques) Ltd. The directors of the company are Spooner and his elderly mother, who takes little active part in the business.

The company operates from a shop in the centre of London. It has banked with your branch for 14 years, and you are currently marking an overdraft limit for working capital purposes of £500,000 secured by a second charge over the shop, a debenture and a guarantee for £80,000 from Spooner. The second charge ranks after a long-term loan from a finance company, currently standing at £89,764. This loan was used to improve the shop.

Spooner's mother has also provided interest-free funds to improve the shop, and these now total £100,000.

The overdraft is due for review. In recent months it has shown little fluctuation, and a hard core of around £400,000 has developed.

Spooner calls to see you, bringing with him his latest accounts in draft form. He asks you to increase the overdraft limit by £200,000 as follows:

(a) £100,000 to acquire some particularly good antique furniture, which he believes he will be able to sell for £175,000 within 6 months; and

(b) £100,000 to repay the loan from his mother, who will soon need part of this money to meet living expenses.

Spooner is a longstanding customer whom the bank would want to help. He has been in the business a long time, and appears to know what he is doing, given the history of profit retentions.

The sales and profits for the business are erratic, but this is a dealing business and the good gross margins suggest Spooner buys and sells well.

However, he does seem to hold his stock for an inordinate amount of time to achieve his prices. The bank has been generous to Spooner in allowing the overdraft to drift up to fund both stock purchases and, one suspects, some of the property improvements. The bank situation is probably becoming a little uncomfortable.

FELIX SPOONER (ANTIQUES) LTD
BALANCE SHEETS

	Year A		Year B		Year C (Draft)	
	£	£	£	£	£	£
Current assets						
Cash	150		146		760	
Debtors	24,344		43,096		43,577	
Stock*	613,925	638,419	676,639	719,881	762,889	807,226
Current liabilities						
Creditors	43 717		65,118		39,677	
Bank overdraft	251817		379,323		458,965	
Loan for repayment within 12 months	34,000		100,000		100,000	
Tax	6,455	(335,989)	-	(544,441)	15,245	(613,887)
		302,430		175,440		193,339
Loans not due for repayment within 12 months		-		(85,444)		(90,939)
Fixed assets						
Freehold property	220,000		405,372		445,406	
Furniture and equipment	1,729	221,729	1,833	407,205	3,930	449,336
Net assets		524,159		497,201		551,736
Financed by:						
Issued share capital		200		200		200
Capital reserve		194,220		194,220		194,220
Profit and loss account		329,739		302,781		357,316
		524,159		497,201		551,736

*Directors' valuation

PROFIT AND LOSS SUMMARY

12 months to	Year A	Year B	Year C (Draft)
	£	£	£
Sales	324,293	224,856	403,879
Purchases	176,430	122,338	158,916
Gross profit	147,863	102,518	244,963
Directors' remuneration	35,000	26,570	37,884
Net profit before tax	29,695	(33,413)	69,707

RATIO ANALYSIS

	Year A	Year B	Year C (Draft)
Current ratio	1.90:1	1.32:1	1.31:1
Acid test	0.07:1	0.08:1	0.07:1
Credit given (days)	27	70	39
Credit taken (days)	90	194	91
Stock turnover (days)	1,270	2,019	1,752
Cross margin (%)	45.6	45.6	60.7
Net margin (%)	9.2	(14.9)	17.3
Net gearing (%)	55	114	118
Interest cover (times)	2.0	0.1	2.2

In this context Spooner's request for an extra £200,000 is unwelcome. The purchase of the furniture makes good sense, if indeed he can move it on at the sort of profit margin he is talking about. Given the fact he seems to know his business, the risk is a marginal one against the value of the furniture.

Similarly, given that the directors' remuneration has been modest, refusing repayment of the mother's loan would be a harsh decision. Some sort of compromise needs to be reached. Spooner has to be forced to sell stock, even if this is done at less than ideal prices. A suitable compromise might include suggesting that the loan to his mother should be paid in instalments.

This would meet both her needs and contain external borrowing, while switching part of the overdraft onto loan with specific reductions would get the borrowing down to a reasonable level by forcing Spooner to institute stock sales in a controlled way. If the bank increased its facilities, would the security position be satisfactory?

Although the charge over the property is only a second mortgage, the first charge on the property is relatively small in relation to its overall value. An up-to-date valuation of the property is necessary, and provided this is near to book value, consideration could even be given to taking out the finance company, which has the first charge.

The other major asset is, of course, the stock. Spooner is in a better position to value this than the bank, but if exposure is being increased to an uncomfortable level, it may be a good idea to commission an independent valuation of the major items.

Provided the property and stock valuations come out near book value, with the addition of a further £100,000 of stock the bank would have £1.2 million of cover for £700,000 of liabilities, even if the mother's loan was repaid in full immediately. By only allowing the mother's loan to be repaid in instalments, there would be approximately twice cover by assets for the bank lending, and it should be tenable in the short term. However, Spooner must be forced to reduce stock to more reasonable levels, and the transfer of the hard core to loan with a fixed reduction programme would be appropriate. It would also be right to have an interest rate loading on the hard core until it is cleared.

Restaurants

9

Any banker who has been in lending for any length of time will not only have lent to finance a restaurant but will also have seen a restaurant business fail. The failure rate of restaurant businesses is extremely high, perhaps the highest of any type of business that bankers are asked to finance.

Why should this be so? There are a number of reasons at the detailed level, but they can fundamentally be put into two main categories:

(a)   The business attracts a lot of 'gifted amateurs': people who think they have the knowledge and skills to run a restaurant. They have eaten at lots of restaurants and they can cook. They have a rough idea of the difference between the cost of a restaurant meal and the cost of its ingredients – so they 'know' there are good profits to be made. But they are basically naïve and see things through 'rose-tinted spectacles'.

(b)   Running a good restaurant is actually very difficult, and requires a lot of business skill. There are many pitfalls to be avoided, and not all of these are immediately obvious. A high level of a particular type of streetwise business acumen is needed. The nature of the basic business risks involved will be discussed below, but the risks are generally high, and top-class management is needed to handle them.

This amalgam of lots of potential restaurant owners with naïve expectations and a requirement for a high level of special management skills is a recipe for lots of failures.

Business risks

Business risk is best described as the combination of the risks that a business faces as it interfaces with its external environment, particularly its market place. It is about things that are hard for the management to control because they are effectively 'givens' in the area in which it operates.

Business risk is high for restaurants because:

(a) *There are low barriers to entry into the business* – New restaurants open and close all the time, and true differentiation is difficult.

(b) *Substitute products are readily available* – People do not have to eat out, they can easily eat at home and will do so, particularly when money is tight.

(c) *Competition in the industry is high* – In most locations there are lots of places to eat out. At the lower end, price competition is fierce, and there are some powerful, large players operating in the business.

(d) *The power of suppliers is high* – Most small restaurants are smaller businesses than their suppliers. If they do not pay their bills on time, their lifeblood of supplies will quickly be cut off, and the supplier will not notice much difference in his turnover.

(e) *The power of buyers is high* – While the customer base is highly fragmented, they usually have lots of options and, if offended, can easily take their business elsewhere. The restaurateur must pay continuous attention to customer satisfaction to be successful.

These things can be managed and risks reduced. Most restaurants will try to differentiate themselves from the competition by having a specific format or by targeting a particular type of customer. Just how effective the differentiation is, or is likely to be, has to be a matter of judgement in each case. For a banker such judgements are not easy, and the existence of a good track record by the restaurateur is likely to be the only effective guide.

Another way in which risk can be ameliorated is through franchising. With the best franchise operations there is a lot of top-class professional help available to the franchisee to get him or her through all the pitfalls. Bankers are therefore generally going to be more supportive of franchise operations where there is a proven format and support.

Management issues

The restaurant business may look relatively simple, but there are many pitfalls for naïve or unwary management. Firm management disciplines need to be put in place and then rigorously followed.

Most of the potential problems, though by no means all, revolve around control of staff. While it is not impossible to run a restaurant as a one-man band or, say, a husband and wife operation, the vast majority employ other staff. Typically, restaurant staff are poorly paid, often part-time, and some will depend on tips for a reasonable income. High rates of staff turnover are not unusual. Maintaining high standards of staff honesty in such circumstances is not easy. Strong financial disciplines and controls are needed to stop 'staff fiddles' eating into profits.

There are three main areas where discipline is vital:

(a)   portion control;

(b)   control of cash;

(c)   standards of hygiene.

Portion control

Portion control is about ensuring that expected gross profit from a sale is in fact achieved. It is therefore a wider issue than simply avoiding staff defalcations. Putting more food on a customer's plate than has been budgeted for is a good way to lose money in any case.

The start point is that there must be a sound budgeting system, which is rigorously implemented. Then performance has to be monitored at the individual meal level so that the portions of food for which revenue is received tally with what has been used as the meal ingredients.

Failure to do this will encourage staff to take advantage of the system — food will disappear from the kitchen and/or portions customers pay for will have the associated revenue disappear into staff pockets with no way of tracking what is happening. Control of high-value items, particularly alcoholic drinks, is vital.

The gifted amateur type of restaurant owner often does not have the extent of these necessary disciplines on his or her radar; and even when they do, do not have the desire or technical knowledge on how to implement them. Serious and detailed questions have to be asked of any prospective restaurateur.

Control of cash

In a business where cash is often used in payment and given to staff other than the proprietor, the possibility of cash 'leakage' is significant. It can never be completely stopped, but it has to be controlled. Here again sound budgeting is the key, so that actual revenue can be compared with what should have been received from sales.

Individual members of staff have to be held accountable for the cash they should have received, and they cannot be retained if a pattern of discrepancies occurs.

The control of cash becomes significantly more difficult when the proprietor is not regularly on the premises – as will be the case when there is more than one outlet. The management of the other outlet has to be trustworthy and be monitored carefully. Collusion between management and staff at remote outlet is a particularly dangerous situation.

Standards of hygiene

Another important area where management control is vital is in ensuring good standards of cleanliness and hygiene.

Restaurants have legal obligations and are subject to regular inspections by the environmental health authorities. Ultimately there is the risk that the business will be closed down if standards are not adequate.

In any case, there is no better way of losing customers quickly than making them ill after eating at your establishment. Word-of-mouth comments get passed around, and suddenly there are no customers. It is extremely difficult to restore a reputation in this area once it has been lost.

Financial risks

Restaurants are exposed to the same financial risks as other businesses, but they are particularly vulnerable to the volume of business they transact because of the nature of their cost structures.

Typically, restaurants have a high fixed-cost base. Premises costs are usually a major expense; the initial capital expenditure for fitting out will be relatively high in relation to likely revenue, and often produces high finance charges. Even staff costs may include a high fixed element: the business cannot operate without a chef, even if waiters can be brought in or let go on a more casual basis.

However, variable costs will form a relatively low portion of revenue received.

It is not untypical to see the cost of a restaurant meal to be more than treble the cost of its food ingredients.

There is a technique for looking at the financial impact of different cost structures and their implications called 'operational gearing'. Operational gearing is associated with break-even analysis and is technically defined as the reciprocal of the margin of safety. In layman's language, it compares the contribution made from sales with fixed costs and the ultimate net profit earned.

A business where the contribution earned on sales is high in relation to the net profit eventually produced is said to be highly operationally geared. Such businesses are particularly risky because a small drop in sales produces a large drop in contribution and quickly produces a position where the business moves from profit to loss. (Conversely, of course, a small rise in sales produces a large rise in net profit.)

Highly operationally geared businesses have potentially very volatile cash flow as sales go up and down. Restaurants have a cost structure that can easily result in their being highly operationally geared. And indeed many of them are – a reason for the high failure rate. They find it hard to survive if sales drop below break-even for anything but a short period of time.

Capacity is a significant issue. A restaurant that only has the capacity to get past break-even at high levels of utilization will be particularly vulnerable as it will not be able to use the good times to build a cash buffer to cover any future downturn.

Not all restaurants are highly operationally geared, but many are. So an analysis of a restaurant business's operational gearing is a valuable tool in assessing the risks involved in lending to it. However, this is easier said than done. Break-even analysis and the calculation of operational gearing is dependent on having a split between fixed and variable costs. Financial accounts split costs between direct and indirect rather than fixed and variable, and financial accounts are usually all the lender has to work with.

Some interpretation of the financial accounting information has to made. Most direct costs tend to be variable while the majority of indirect are fixed. Judgement is needed, because direct labour in a restaurant can effectively be fixed, while gas and electricity may be variable. But comparing an adjusted gross profit margin with the net margin probably gives a reasonable proxy for operational gearing. Where a large GP% produces a small NP%, there is probably high potential for cash flow volatility. Lending on the basis that a stable cash flow from profits is going to be available to pay down borrowing in such a business could be fraught with danger.

Case 1

Ben and Bill Burger are brothers, both in their late 30s. Five years ago they set up a new company, Best Burgers Ltd. They each injected £10,000 into the company: £5,000 as share capital and £5,000 as loan capital.

The company was granted a 20-year lease of a unit in Brown Street at an annual rent of £7,500, reviewable every five years. The Burgers developed the unit into a fast food restaurant, selling mainly hamburgers. Towards the end of Year A the Burgers completed the development of a second unit in Green Road; a 20-year lease was granted at a rent of £8,500 per annum, also reviewable every five years.

The company has banked with you since it was incorporated. Five years ago you agreed an overdraft facility of £7,500, secured by a first charge over the lease and the unlimited joint and several guarantees of the Burgers. In September Year A, during the development of the Green Road unit, you increased the facility to £15,000 and renewed at this figure last September. The account has operated within the arrangements, and for the past nine months has run in credit.

Last week the Burgers arranged an appointment with you for today. They left with your secretary the audited accounts for the year ending 31 May Year C, which they had just received from the auditor.

At today's meeting they explain that they have the opportunity to purchase another fast food restaurant in Grey Lane. This unit has been trading for three years, and sales there are currently averaging £3,000 per week. The lease has 17 years to run, with a current rent of £9,000 per annum to be reviewed in September Year E. The condition of the unit and the equipment is good; the Burgers would not expect any major expenditure at Grey Lane for at least three years.

The asking price, to include the lease, goodwill, fixtures and fittings, is £90,000, but the Burgers are confident that they can negotiate a reduction of £5,000. Over recent months the company's bank account has been showing credit balances of over £30,000. Allowing for the £15,000 overdraft facility, the Burgers require a loan of £50,000 to complete the purchase of the unit.

You question the brothers on the current performance of their existing units. They expect sales for the year to increase by 12% over the last year; direct costs and wages will increase in line with sales, but overhead expenses and rates are budgeted to increase at 10%. The brothers' remuneration will be £15,000 per annum each, and they wish to make a further contribution of £10,000 into the pension fund.

Best Burgers Limited is a relatively recently established business, which wishes to expand by purchasing a third unit. Making the credit assessment is somewhat easier than in the previous two cases because there is a track record of performance. The Burgers have been successful. Starting up this kind of fast food outlet from scratch is not easy, and the fact that the business has made profits almost from the start is a good sign. The brothers have already shown that they can expand the business by acquiring a second unit in Year B and, although this obviously started slowly, a good sales performance in Year C shows their capacity to develop the business. The good progress the business has made can be judged by the level of retentions, which needs to be looked at in terms of both net worth and directors' loans, as these two items represent the total proprietors' capital. The overall capital base of the business has grown from £23,600 in Year A to £50,500 in Year C, which is a creditable performance. There can therefore be some confidence in the management.

It is particularly comforting to note that, despite substantial capital expenditure on the restaurants, the business has been able to improve its cash position to the point where in Year C there was no net borrowing.

The new unit the brothers wish to acquire is already established, so it would be

BEST BURGERS LTD
BALANCE SHEET

As at 31 May	Year A		Year B		Year C	
	£000	£000	£000	£000	£000	£000
Fixed assets						
Leasehold improvements		11.9		21.1		17.9
Fixtures and fittings		17.9		30.1		25.5
Motor vehicles		8.0		6.0		4.5
		37.8		57.2		47.9
Cash	1.3		1.8		15.6	
Debtors	2.1		3.1		3.3	
Stock	7.1		12.8		14.8	
	10.5		17.7		33.7	
Creditors – trade	7.6		12.7		16.2	
– others	5.4		8.1		10.4	
Bank	2.4		10.9		–	
Hire purchase	9.3		11.1		4.5	
Directors' loans	10.0		12.3		10.9	
	34.7		55.1		42.0	
Net current liabilities		(24.2)		(37.4)		(8.3)
Net tangible assets		13.6		19.8		39.6
Financed by:						
Share capital		10.0		10.0		10.0
Profit and loss		3.6		9.8		29.6
		13.6		19.8		39.6
Sales – Brown Street		112.3		125.9		145.2
– Green Road		–		66.4		135.0
Gross profit		73.0		121.0		174.3
Wages		25.8		46.8		64.1
Rent/rates		10.6		20.8		23.4
Overhead expenses		7.0		13.3		16.9
Finance costs		2.0		5.0		4.8
Directors' remuneration		18.0		19.2		26.2
Pension contribution		–		–		10.0
Depreciation		6.0		9.7		9.1
Net profit		3.6		6.2		19.8

RATIOS AND OTHER INFORMATION

	Year A	Year B	Year C
Current ratio	0.30:1	0.32:1	0.80:1
Acid test	0.10:1	0.09:1	0.45:1
Credit given (days)	7	6	4
Credit taken (days)	71	65	56
Stock turnover (days)	66	66	51
Gross margin (%)	65.0	62.9	62.2
Net margin (%)	3.2	3.2	7.1
Interest cover (times)	2.8	2.2	5.1
Net gearing (%)	44	66	
(Directors' loans as capital)			

BUDGET FOR NEXT 12 MONTHS

	Existing £000	outlets £000	New £000	outlet £000	Combined £000	outlets £000
Sales		313		156		469
Direct costs	119		60		179	
Wages	71	190	36	96	107	286
		123		60		183
Rent	16		9		25	
Finance costs			9		10	
New outlet manager	–		15		15	
Depreciation	9		10		19	
Directors' remuneration	40		–		40	
Other overheads	27	93	15	58	42	151
Net profit		30		2		32
Gross profit (%)		62		62		62
Net profit (%)		9.6		1.3		6.8
Interest cover (times)		31		1.2		4.2

appropriate to see some sort of figures relating to its performance. The brothers themselves ought to have seen such figures as, despite their experience, the current performance of the Grey Lane outlet will be of importance in establishing both the reasonableness of the purchase price and the figures that they have budgeted.

Is the purchase price of £90,000 reasonable? What proportion of the £90,000 represents the value of the lease and fixtures and fittings? Given that the lease of Grey Lane will be reviewed in the not-too-distant future, it will not have a particularly high value. The Grey Lane restaurant appears to be roughly the same size as the Burgers' existing outlets, so fixtures and fittings are probably not going to be worth much more than £12,000–£15,000. It looks therefore as though the goodwill element will be around £70,000. If the finance costs relating to the new outlet are added back to the net profit, it would appear that the initial contribution that the new outlet will make to the overall Best Burgers Ltd business is £11,000 per annum, which suggests that the brothers are paying about 6.5 times annual profits, which looks a bit steep. This will give them a return on their overall investment of £90,000 of approximately 12.5%, which looks a bit thin for a business that will involve them in a lot of work. However, they seem to know what they are doing, and there could well be capacity to expand the business further to improve the return. A hidden issue in this sort of proposition is always the amount of cash that the proprietors are able to take out of the till. This will of course increase their real return and make the acquisition more sensible.

The £70,000 of goodwill will have a major impact on the Best Burgers Ltd balance sheet, creating a negative net worth position. Obviously, things will look a little better if the brothers are indeed able to negotiate a £5,000 reduction in the asking price but, even so, it would appear that the bank will be providing facilities of £65,000 against a balance sheet deficit.

This may be tenable as the budget figures for the next 12 months ought to be achievable. With overall depreciation and net profit totalling £51,000 in a business where creditors have always been able to provide more than sufficient finance for working capital needs, there should be a strong cash flow. The new outlet will need to be tightly controlled as it will be run by a 'non-family' manager. The brothers will have to ensure that any cash taken out of the till does not 'leak' into the manager's pocket rather than their own, or they could easily see their profits eliminated. Having to control an outlet in this way is a new departure for them, so it will be appropriate to establish what monitoring procedures they are putting in place.

Given the balance sheet deficit and the risks involved in the new outlet, it would probably be appropriate to have good security. The leases of the restaurants will not supply this, and it may well be appropriate to seek support for the Burgers' guarantees, perhaps on the basis that this support will be released after 12 months provided overall performance comes up to scratch. Keyman cover, and perhaps health insurance for the brothers, would also be appropriate. This proposition has a lot going for it, but there are risks for the lender. In trying to run an outlet outside their own direct control the brothers are taking a risk, and they are paying what appears to be a fairly steep price for Grey Lane, which has a considerable adverse impact on their balance sheet. Everything about the brothers' past history suggests that they will be successful, but a lender is not taking a proprietor's risk, and I believe a prudent bank manager would insist on good tangible security before agreeing the facilities.

Case 2

Simpkins Chop Joint Limited owns 15 restaurants in city centres across the UK. The restaurants have a standard menu ranging from hamburgers and mixed grills to chicken and steaks. The average sale per customer last year was £16.

The business was established 20 years ago by the current proprietor, Alan Jarvis, who is in his late 50s and has worked in the restaurant trade all his working life. At first the company thrived, but in recent years, with the advent of new restaurant formats, competition has increased and business has not been easy. The company's premises are all short leaseholds held on fully repairing and insuring terms. Most of them are subject to upwards-only rent reviews.

As the general UK economy has improved, the company's business has picked up, and it is now trading profitably following a period of losses. However, during the period of difficult trading, capital expenditure had to be cut back, and some restaurants are in need of refurbishment.

Jarvis believes that the company has turned the corner, and would like to spend £300,000 on capital expenditure on the restaurants. He also has his eye on acquiring two new sites, which would cost a total of £500,000 to buy and fit out.

The company banks with one of your competitors, where it has an overdraft limit of £500,000 and term loans, totalling £235,000, repayable at £35,000 per quarter. The bank has a fixed and floating charge over the assets of the company.

Jarvis calls to see you. He tells you that, despite the fact that he has stuck faithfully to his arrangements with his current bank and his overdraft shows a full fluctuation, the bank has refused to advance the company the extra funds it now needs. He asks you to consider taking over the existing facilities and agreeing to two new term loans – £300,000 over 5 years for capital expenditure, and £500,000 over 10 years for the restaurant purchases.

SIMPKINS CHOP JOINT LIMITED
BALANCE SHEETS

As at 30 September	Audited Year A £000	£000	Draft Year B £000	£000
Current assets				
Cash	1		1	
Debtors	86		68	
Prepayments - Rent	451		468	
Rates	118		468	
Other	39		76	
Stock	61	756	76	777
Current liabilities				
Bank overdraft	251		177	
Bank loans	375		235	
Trade creditors	695		804	
Rent creditors	596		535	
Other creditors	658	317		
VAT	87		90	
Current tax	60		240	
Prior year's tax (refund)	(63)	(2,659)	–	(2,398)
Net current liabilities		(1,903)		(1,621)
Fixed assets				
Leasehold premises	1096	1,038		
Equipment, fixtures and fittings	1081	2,177	952	1,990
Deferred taxation		(156)		(88)
Net assets		118		281
Financed by:				
Share capital		300		300
Profit and loss account		(182)		(19)
		118		281

PROFIT AND LOSS ACCOUNT

Year to 30 September	Audited Year A £000	Draft Year B £000	Forecast Year C £000
Turnover	6,653	7,341	8,856
Variable costs			
Food	2,095	2,296	2,789
Restaurant wages	928	947	1,192
Catering equipment	78	98	115
Credit card charges	59	61	83
	3,160	3,402	4179
Gross profit	3,493	3,939	4,677
Fixed costs			
Publicity	5	5	10
Administrative salaries	118	122	128
Rent	1,879	1,947	2,081
Rates	476	542	610
Maintenance and services	398	419	446
Directors' remuneration	45	50	60
Depreciation	382	368	373
Interest	83	71	72
Other expenses	55	59	66
	3,441	3,583	3,846
Profit before tax	52	356	831
Corporation tax	201	193	321
Profit after tax	(149)	(163)	(510)

ACCOUNTING RATIOS

	Year A	Year B	Forecast Year C
Food and drink purchases (% of sales)	31.5	31.3	31.5
Restaurant wages (% of sales)	13.9	12.9	13.5
Gross margin (%)	52.5	53.7	52.8
Net margin (%)	1.0	4.8	9.4
Interest cover (times)	1.6	6.0	12.5
Net gearing (%)	530	146	–
Current ratio	0.28:1	0.32:1	–
Acid test	0.26:1	0.29:1	–
Credit taken (days)	121	128	–
Stock turnover (days)	11	12	–

This business is being offered from another bank so caution is necessary, particularly as the situation seems to have been a problem for the current bankers.

The company has been around a long time under its present management, so there is a clear track record. The proprietor is experienced if a little 'long in the tooth'. His management style needs to be understood – in particular, how he deals with controlling the local management of the individual restaurants in a business notorious for cash 'leakages'. In view of his age, what succession plans are there?

The restaurant format looks jaded, and Jarvis seems to have no plans to update it. The return to profitability seems to have more to do with the general economic upturn than any management action. Moreover, Jarvis , with his simple strategy of expansion, does not appear willing to acknowledge there is any kind of problem.

The Year B accounts are draft – how accurate have draft accounts proved in the past? The improvement in gross margin in Year B is a solid achievement at the same time as a 10.3% increase in sales. However, it seems largely as a result of suppressing a rise in wages – something that is not expected to continue, as indicated in the forecast.

The business has a high fixed-cost base – probably higher than the overheads alone, as restaurant wages are probably a fixed cost in the short term. The major overheads – rent and rates – are outside management control and are increasing. The business is therefore very sensitive to sales volumes. Some crude sensitivity analysis demonstrates this. Taking the expected overhead increase of £263,000 and say half the projected wages increase (say £122,000), it can be seen that the business would not be profitable in Year C at Year B sales levels.

The bank needs to see a breakdown for individual restaurants so that the effects of closing or selling the poorer performers can be established. Having said this, the flexibility to exit an individual restaurant may not exist in practice. The possibility would be heavily dependent on the willingness to accept the surrender of a lease if it could not be sold.

Net gearing has reduced significantly because, although profits are not particularly high, the heavy depreciation charge allows a sufficient level of cash flow to reduce borrowing significantly in the absence of commensurate capital expenditure. Even so, the capital base is low to sustain sales of £7-8 million. There is evidence of tight liquidity, and the length of credit being taken looks excessive for foodstuff purchases. A significant portion of rents – which are usually payable in advance – is shown as creditors, suggesting they are in arrears.

Given the level of turnover and low capital base, an overdraft limit of £500,000 is probably on the low side of the actual need. The capital expenditure is likely to be desirable, and the proposed term is probably about right. But the proposal to buy more outlets looks unnecessarily risky given the business's past history.

The only security available is the leases and fixtures and fittings. The leases will have little value in a break-up as they are likely to contain bankruptcy clauses. However, a good receiver would probably be able to raise a reasonable sum by selling the business as a going concern, given its history and the receiver's ability to retain only the profitable outlets.

The long-term viability of this business depends on its sales performance being maintained or improved. Given the management complacency and the lack of cash to change the format, there must be a real possibility that sales will drop back again when market conditions become less favourable. The probability is that the current bank is being sensible in trying to drive the business away. The right decision would be to refuse the opportunity to take on the account.

Case 3

Domino Corleone has had an account with your bank for 20 years. Both he and his wife, Renata, are aged 45. Mr Corleone is the sole proprietor of a restaurant called 'The Godfather's Place', which is located in a street adjacent to the High Road in your area. The premises are subject to a 17-year lease, which is charged to the bank.

Some five years ago, you agreed a loan of £40,000 to enable your customer to buy out his brother, Michael. Currently there is nearly £10,000 still to pay on this loan. Mr and Mrs Corleone's matrimonial home was charged when the loan was agreed, at which time there was an equity of £55,000 after a building society mortgage.

Having visited the restaurant, you are aware that there are 25 tables with 82 places available. The premises are open seven evenings per week, and at lunch times on Monday to Saturday. Weekends are invariably heavily booked, and there is good trade throughout the week. Mr Corleone has considerable assistance from his son and daughter at weekends, and from his wife on a full-time basis.

As well as the bank loan, the business enjoys an overdraft limit of £15,000.

The business also has support from other members of the Corleone family, and the creditors figure in the last accounts included £48,000 of loans from the family.

Corleone calls to see you. He will shortly have the opportunity to acquire the freehold of his premises, as it is to be auctioned. Based on prices achieve for similar nearby units, Corleone believes he will have to offer £170,000. He requests another loan, for the full purchase price, repayable over 20 years.

D CORLEONE trading as 'THE GODFATHER'S PLACE'
TRADING AND PROFIT AND LOSS ACCOUNT

12 months to 30 June	£	Year A £	£	Year B £	£	Year C £
Sales		207,998		206,442		228,765
Less cost of sales		(65,482)		(66,000)		(70,112)
Gross profit		142,516		140,441		158,653
Expenses						
Wages	42,119		40,680		43,228	
Finance	14,341		13,040		12,329	
Rent	27,000		27,390		28,900	
Rates/water	6,248		6,360		6,595	
Light/heat	7,746		6,744		6,934	
Other expenses	13,309	(110,763)	15,634	(109,848)	21,895	(119,881)
Net profit		31,753		30,593		38,772

BALANCE SHEETS

As at 30 June	Year A £	Year A £	Year B £	Year B £	Year C £	Year C £
Current assets						
Cash at bank	1,547		294		109	
Stock	4,982	6,529	5,147	5,441	5,000	5,109
Current liabilities						
Creditors	68,739		64,237		66,986	
Bank overdraft	11,712	(80,451)	11,947	(76,184)	18,131	(85,117)
Net current liabilities		(73,922)		(70,743)		(80,008)
Fixed assets						
Lease	60,000		60.000		60,000	
Fixtures and fittings	9,800		9,200		9,400	
Motor vehicle	1,300		1,000		15,809	
Goodwill	70,000	141,000	70,000	140,200	70,000	155,209
Medium-term loan		(29,622)		(21,648)		(12,213)
		37,556		47,809		62,988
Capital account						
Balance brought forward		22,429	37,556	47,809		
Add profit		31,753		30,593		38,772
		54,182		68,149		86,581
Less drawings		(16,626)		(20,340)		(23,593)
Balance carried forward		37,556		47,809		62,988

ACCOUNTING RATIOS

	Year A	Year B	Year C
Net gearing (%) (not adjusted for goodwill)	106	70	48
Gross margin (%)	68.5	68.0	69.4
Net margin (%)	15.2	14.8	16.9
Interest cover (times)	3.2	3.3	4.1

BANK ACCOUNT

	High £	Low £	Average £	Limit £
Year A	14,913 Dr	5,906 Dr	8,316 Dr	15,000
Year B	12,030 Dr	2,917 Dr	5,707 Dr	15,000
Year C	15,130 Dr	6,332 Dr	8,200 Dr	15,000

This is a longstanding customer whom the bank would wish to help. The business is well established and seems to have a loyal customer base. Previous arrangements with the bank appear to have been honoured. (The balance sheet appears to show a small excess – but this looks to be due to a vehicle purchase, which should probably be financed by means other than the overdraft.)

Management has been satisfactory to get the business into its current good position. The help from within the family has been important – are they paid and will the children continue the current arrangement?

The purchase of the freehold is an acceptable purpose, and it is probably a good idea given the annual rent rises.

The business has no capital base if the goodwill is discounted. However, the consistent profit performance suggests that the goodwill does have a value. The gearing ratio really ought to be calculated after deducting goodwill – but in its shown form does show a steadily strengthening capital structure.

The substantially negative net current asset position suggests that the business is illiquid, but the position is being sustained by the money loaned from within the family. From the bank's point of view, these loans ought to be formally subordinated.

Profitability has been excellent, and the profits have been retained within the business.

The proposition is for a £170,000 loan over 20 years. At say 11%, the repayments would amount to £20,910 per annum on a fully amortizing basis. This is less than the current rent. So, although advancing 100% of the requirement is less than ideal, the proposition is a good one in cash flow terms. Indeed, a more aggressive repayment schedule would be possible.

The property would need to be valued on a freehold basis. One result of the purchase will be to apparently weaken the balance even more. This is because the nominal value of the lease of £60,000 will disappear. This should not be taken too seriously because the true value of the business rests in its ability to generate cash in the future, and the freehold purchase actually strengthens this.

The bank should retain a second charge over the matrimonial home to keep a security margin. It would also be appropriate to formally subordinate the family loans. Subject to these conditions, the loan should be agreed.

Farmers

10

Most bankers tend to be urban creatures, and of all the specialist types of business to which they are ask to lend, farming probably fills them with the highest degree of trepidation. There is a mystique about farming advances, the assessment of which involves special documents such as farmers' balance sheets, and unusual terms and techniques such as rental equivalent.

In reality, there is no need for this degree of unease. Farmers are relatively typical small businessmen/women, and pose very similar problems to the lender as do other small businesses. Farmers do not, for example, enjoy paying tax, and their financial accounts tend to reflect this to the same extent as those of retailers or small manufacturers. Fundamentally, there is no need to treat farmers as being 'different'.

Chapter 12 of *Bankers' Lending Techniques* covers the theoretical way for dealing with farming advances in some detail, and the following remarks need to be read in conjunction with that chapter. The fundamental issues to be addressed when looking at farming lending propositions are the same as for any other:

(a) whether the proposed borrowing can be repaid on the basis of the story being put forward by the farmer;

(b) what the situation for the lender will be if things go unexpectedly wrong, as they undoubtedly can in a business like farming which can be heavily affected by outside factors, such as adverse weather conditions.

Serviceability

With a 'normal' business, a lender will expect a new lending proposition to be accompanied by a business plan, including budgets, cash flow forecasts and so on, and an indication of the assumptions on which the plan is based. The lender then needs to test the assumptions to see if the plan is viable. This testing has to be carried out on what has to be essentially a commonsense basis, with a lender using any local or specialist knowledge available, but particularly comparing what is forecast to happen with the business's past track record. There is absolutely no reason why this approach should not be adopted with farmers.

The businesslike farmer will appreciate the importance of formal planning systems, and will have a cropping/stocking plan on which the financial budgets and cash flow forecasts can be based. The cropping/stocking plan will provide the major underlying assumption that will have to be tested, such as whether the land can produce the expected yields, and this is where local knowledge will play a significant part. But even if a lender does not have detailed local knowledge, there will still be the firm evidence of the farm's past track record of production against which to examine the forecast.

Even if a farmer has difficulty in producing a financial plan, there are plenty of organizations that will help, including the farming departments of the main banks. However, no matter who produces the forecasts, performance will depend on the farmer's experience and track record. Past performance always provides the best guide to the future, and an analysis of historical financial data when combined with a visit to the farm will give a strong indication of the farmer's management ability. Here again, the approach being adopted is very similar to that used for, say, lending to a manufacturer, where a visit to the factory and an examination of the historical financial performance will provide the best basis for assessing the ability of a business's management to achieve forecasts.

The farmer's projections must reflect the underlying nature of his business. Not all farm enterprises are the same. For example, there will be a different budgetary and cash flow product cycle for a dairy compared with that for an arable farmer. Receipts from milk sales have traditionally been received monthly from the Milk Marketing Board, while corn is harvested in the autumn and, although it can be stored for later sale, has a basic annual cycle. Lambs, similarly, are produced annually, and wool is sheared annually. In relation to other meat production, pigs can probably be turned into cash within three months, but beef cattle might take as long as two years to be sold. Of course, many farm enterprises pursue a number of different activities, and this will further complicate the budgeting process.

Although good financial planning should be the norm, in company with many small businessmen some farmers are primarily interested in the production side of their business, and it can be difficult to get meaningful plans out of them, even with all the help available. This is where the concept of rental equivalent can be helpful in testing serviceability. Different types of farm enterprise can generate different levels of fundamental profitability per acre. Land quality may be different, enabling high yields in some areas compared with others, and different types of enterprise will involve a different level of intensity of land use, and hence profitability per acre. The rental equivalent reflects the sort of contribution that each acre can reasonably be expected to make towards meeting rent (if any), finance charges and capital repayments. It thus reflects the financial pressure under which a particular farm enterprise may reasonably be expected to operate. It needs to be firmly understood that rental equivalent is not a substitute for a realistic budget and cash flow forecast, which ought to provide the most accurate assessment of a farm's capacity to sustain financial pressure through looking at the individual items of revenue and expenditure in detail. By comparison, rental equivalent is a very crude and 'broad brush' test that nevertheless, can provide a simple rule of thumb when no formal plan, or one that may be considered unreliable, has been produced.

Protection against downside risk

Even with the benefit of the farm support that the EU's Common Agricultural Policy gives, farmers are more exposed than most businessmen to factors outside their control. Even the best farmer may be caught out by particularly adverse weather conditions or be hit by a livestock disease requiring the slaughter of all the farm's animals. A most dramatic illustration of an unforeseen outside factor that had a major impact on certain farmers was the Chernobyl nuclear power station disaster in the former Soviet Union. The radiation from the consequent radioactive cloud contaminated pasture land in the UK and, more or less overnight, made it impossible for many hill farmers to sell their stock. While this is a fairly extreme example, it does illustrate the kind of thing that can go wrong, against which a lender will want to be protected.

The best form of protection a lender can have is a strong capital position within the farm and/or good security cover. The best form of security a farmer can give is a charge over the farm itself, assuming the land is freehold. For a long time after the Second World War, farm land prices were on a continuously rising trend. Against this background, there was a tendency to permit some farmers to borrow beyond a level they could reasonably expect to service. This allowed a position to develop whereby many over-borrowed farmers found that their net capital position increased, even when they were making trading losses, simply because of rising land values. In recent years there has been a decline in the value of farm land, and this has emphasized the need for less weight to be given to its present value as security. However, there is no escaping the fact that having a good security margin gives a banker a great deal of comfort when lending to farmers.

Obtaining an up-to-date view of a farmer's net worth is sometimes not very easy. Farmers are notorious for not producing up-to-date accounts, so looking at the last set of audited figures may not be a tremendous help in assessing the present position. As has been indicated above, it is very common for farmers' accounts to be produced 'for the tax man' so that land, buildings and machinery could well be undervalued, as could be stock.

One way of avoiding this problem is to insist on an up-to-date farmer's balance sheet. This is sometimes also known as a farmer's confidential statement. In practice, this is very often filled in by the bank manager from the information given to him by his farming customer, and most banks have their own form of farmer's balance sheet. It is basically a management document that is an up-to-date statement of the farmer's assets and liabilities. The stock and crops on the farm are valued at up-to-date figures (ideally checked with figures provided by *Farmers' Weekly* or other agricultural journals). When the values of land, buildings and machinery and other assets and liabilities are included, an up-to-date net worth position for the farmer can be deduced. If the farmer's balance sheets are taken at different times in the year, the movement in asset values against money owed to the bank can be tracked.

Ideally, on a conservative basis, bank borrowing should not be allowed to exceed 50% of the value of net current assets, although there will obviously be instances where it may be appropriate to exceed this figure.

Case 1

....

Peter Wood is a local farmer who currently banks with a competitor bank. He has now apparently fallen out with them over a matter of poor service. His accountant, who has been a good source of business for you, has telephoned to ask if you would be interested in acquiring Wood's account. You agree to meet Wood at his farm, and the accountant has let you have copies of the latest available balance sheets, although these are two years old.

During your discussions with Mr Wood you learn the following:

(a)   He is aged 42, married, with two boys aged 10 and 12.

(b)   He farms 180 acres, of which 80 acres are owned and 100 acres are rented.

(c)   The farm system consists of a high-yielding dairy herd of 80 cows, with sufficient dairy followers to supply 20 heifers per year (i.e. 20 replacement units), and arable land for growing winter wheat and winter barley.

(d)   His milk quota is adequate for present yield levels.

(e)   An Agricultural Mortgage Corporate (AMC) loan of £40,000 (at 13% p.a. interest) was agreed two years ago for the purchase of 40 acres of land, the term of the loan being 20 years.

(f)   Mr Wood's father granted him an unsecured loan of £15,000 seven years ago. No repayments of capital are required but interest is paid at a fixed rate of 10% per annum.

The owner of 10 of the 100 acres of land that Mr Wood rents has recently died. The executors have offered this land, together with an adjoining 20 acres on which there is vacant possession, to Mr Wood for £30,000. Mr Wood can find £5,000 from his own resources, and so he requires a loan of £25,000 to complete the purchase. Mr Wood asks if your bank would agree to such a request.

You question Mr Wood on the performance of the farm. Last year's dairy herd achieved a gross margin of £550 per cow, while his crops averaged a yield of 2.5 tons per acre. This year he is expecting a gross margin of £580 per head from his 80 cows and £250 per head from the 20 replacement units. With the additional land, he will grow 50 acres of winter wheat at a gross margin of £180 per acre and 20 acres of winter barley at a gross margin of £160 per acre.

Mr Wood estimates his current expenses are as follows:

	£
Wages	10,000
Rent and rates	4,500
General overhead expenses (including depreciation)	17,000

No allowance has been made in these figures for finance costs.

You have walked round the farm with Mr Wood and gained a good impression both of him and of his farm. You are of the opinion that the 80 acres of land Mr Wood currently owns are worth about £1,800 per acre with the benefit of a milk quota, while the new land (i.e. 30 acres, without quota) should be worth about £1,200 per acre. You are aware that cows have an average market value of £550 and replacement units of £600 per head at current prices.

Whenever a business seeks to switch from another bank caution is needed but, in this instance, the introduction is coming from a good and well-known source and the reason given for the proposed transfer is plausible.

Wood seems to know what he is doing, and the farm visit suggests that it is well run. However, Wood does not seem to be the sort of farmer who sets his plans down on paper. The accounts are out of date and there are no management figures. The fact that he can find £5,000 from within his own resources is a good sign, but the £25,000 he is requesting does not seem to allow for any extra costs such as legal fees and so on. It could be that additional expenditure might be required on the new land to bring it up to the same standard as his own. Moreover, to make full use of the land Wood might need to purchase an extra milk quota, and it would be unusual if there was no requirement for some sort of working capital facility. Wood will have to be questioned in some detail on these issues.

Despite the fact that the accounts are out of date, some deductions can be made by combining the information in the last balance sheet with that given verbally by Wood to establish a crude farmer's balance sheet.

PETER WOOD, FARMER
BALANCE SHEETS

As at 30 September	Year A £	Year A £	Year B £	Year B £
Freehold land		71,000		71,000
Tenants' improvements		4,000		3,000
Machinery/plant		22,000		20,000
Motor vehicles		5,000		5,000
		102,000		99,000
Cash	6,000		–	
Debtors/prepayments	12,000		7,000	
Stock – livestock	28,000		30,000	
feed, crops, fertilizer	11,000	57,000	25,000	62,000
		159,000		161,000
Creditors	10,000		3,000	
Bank	–		2,000	
AMC	40,000		38,000	
Mr Wood senior	15,000	65,000	15,000	58,000
Net assets		94,000		103,000
Capital account				
Balance forward	86,000		94,000	
Profit for year	20,000		22,000	
Drawings	(12,000)		(13,000)	
		94,000		103,000
Sales		82,000		88,000
Gross profit		48,500		52,000
Net profit		20,000		22,000
After depreciation		4,000		4,000

RATIOS

	Year A	Year B
Net gearing (%)	52	53
Gross profit margin (%)	59	59
Net profit margin (%)	24	25

CAPITAL BASE

	£	£
Year B balance sheet net assets		103,000
Hidden reserve in land		
80 acres @ £1,800	144,000	
Less balance sheet figure	71,000	73,000
Reserve in stock		
80 cows @ £550	44,000	
20 replacements @ £600	12,000	
	56,000	
Less balance sheet figure	30,000	26,000
		202,000

To this figure could be added the loan from Wood's father, which is quasi-capital, to give an adjusted capital base of £217,000. This would suggest gearing at 27% (or 18% if the father's loan is treated as capital). This is a very acceptable position, although some consideration needs to be given to the potential position if Wood's father were to die and the £15,000 loan had to be repaid.

It is not possible from the figures given to say definitely whether borrowing can be covered twice by net current assets. However, assuming the AMC loan has reduced by £2,000 since the last balance sheet date to £36,000, total outside borrowing would be £61,000. Although the AMC loan is showing on the balance sheet as a current liability, the fact that it is repayable over 20 years suggests that it ought not to be treated as such. This would give a Year B net current asset position of £42,000, to which could be added the hidden reserve in stock of £26,000, suggesting a present net current asset position of £68,000. The position is therefore nearer 100% than 50%, but this need not be of undue concern, given that all the borrowing will be long-term and has arisen largely for the purchase of fixed assets.

Ideally, a lender would wish to see a longer trend than two years' accounts, but sales are showing a satisfactory increase at 6% and the gross margin is stable at 59%. Overheads appear to be well controlled, and the net profit margin has increased slightly between the two years. Again, although Wood has not produced a full budget, one can be deduced. So after drawings of, say, £15,000 (£13,000 in Year B) there will still be a margin of over £4,000 for contingencies and further investment, or additional capital repayment.

BUDGET

	Year A £	Year B £
Projected income (based on expected gross margins):		
80 dairy cows @ £580		46,400
20 replacements @ £250		5,000
50 acres winter wheat @ £180		9,000
20 acres winter barley @ £160		3,200
		63,600
Estimated expenses (before finance costs)		31,500
		32,100
Present finance costs (interest only)		
AMC £36,000 (£2,000 repaid last year) @ 13%	4,680	
Bank overdrafts say £2,000 @ 13%	260	
Father: £15,000 @ 10%	1.500	6.440
		25,660
AMC capital repayments		2,000
		23,660
Additional finance costs:		
10-year bank loan (interest & capital) £25,000 @ 3/Base – 13%	4,450	
Additional working capital say 3/Base – 13% on, say £1,000 overdraft	130	4,580
		19,080

The venture can be tested by looking at the rental equivalent as follows:

	£
Present finance costs	6,440
Additional finance costs	4,580
AMC repayments	2,000
Rent & rates	4,500
	17,520

With 200 acres (excluding the 10 acres of woodland), the rental equivalent is £88 per acre compared with £66 per acre in Year B. At £88 per acre, Wood will probably have to achieve above-average yields for a mixed dairy and arable farm. The enterprise is predominantly dependent on dairying, with 80% of projected gross profit coming from this source so, on the very rough rule-of-thumb guide that rental equivalent gives, repayment should be acceptable.

As security, a first charge on the land to be acquired will be appropriate: £1,200 x 30 acres = £36,000. (The difference between the value of £36,000 and the £30,000 cost is accounted for because Wood is a sitting tenant on part of the land.) Life cover over Wood would also be essential.

There should be little difficulty in agreeing this loan. Repayment looks feasible on both the budget and rental equivalent bases. There is also adequate security. However, it is not immediately apparent where Wood's £5,000 is coming from, and it is likely that there may be significant other expenditure, including the working capital, which needs to be explored. Agreement to, say, a £5,000 overdraft limit should not be a problem, but a higher figure would probably require extra security support, but this is available in the form of a substantial equity in the present land.

Case 2

∙∙

You have been manager of your branch since January Year C. Your predecessor told you on your arrival at the branch that one of his struggling farmer customers was John England. In March Year C you visited the farm as a matter of urgency as the current account had been running without a sanctioned limit for four years; this necessitated frequent reports to your regional office.

Following your visit, the hardcore borrowing of £100,000 was funded to a 20-year capital loan, and an overdraft limit of £10,000 was agreed. Excesses occurred on the current account in September Year C, and when the overdraft reached £33,000 in March Year D, you again visited Moor Farm to complete a confidential farmer's balance sheet. A summary is given below, together with balance sheets for the three years ending 31 March Year C. The net worth of £148,050 in the confidential statement is £20,000 less than that completed in March Year C. You told Mr England that the bank was not prepared to increase its support.

Until Year A, your customer was a dairy and sheep farmer but, in an endeavour to reverse his unprofitability, he decided to venture into raising beef cattle. As a result, turnover rose but so also did losses. Mr England is not unreasonable but he is convinced that eventually 'things will work out'. You do not share his opinion, and in this morning's clearing is his cheque for £5,000 payable to a local merchant. Since March, the lowest overdraft on the current account was £29,000 and the highest £33,500.

This is very much a recovery situation. Mr England is an over-optimistic farmer who is now out of his depth. The switch from dairy/sheep into raising beef cattle has not been justified by any sort of plan or figures to show that this would improve profitability. The bank account is already substantially over the £10,000 overdraft limit, and the issue of the £5,000 cheque to a local merchant shows that either England is cavalier in his approach or, more likely, has poor monitoring systems. In a nutshell, John England is not a particularly businesslike farmer.

In allowing the present situation to develop the bank has been both very generous to and very tolerant of England. The fact that the overdraft has been allowed to get to £32,500 against an overdraft limit of £10,000, even before the arrival of the £5,000 cheque, ought to raise an eyebrow or two at regional office. Obviously the borrowing has been allowed to drift up because there is adequate security in the land and buildings. Assuming that the latest valuation at £208,500 is fair, it suggests that there is a 35% margin in the value of the security. However, there are dangers in lending to a less-than-viable enterprise purely against security values. If anything should happen to the price of farm land, which would cause a drop in the security value, then the bank would be in an awkward position.

England's audited accounts do not show the true position of the farm. The land is in the balance sheet at only £35,000, so there is a hidden reserve of around £173,000. Even so, gearing is around 100%. Liquidity is worsening. Although the current ratio between Year C and Year D seems roughly the same, a large part of the bank borrowing (£98,000) went 'below the line' in Year D, and so has been removed from current liabilities, suggesting a further significant deterioration in the liquid position.

Profitability is non-existent, and the difference between the confidential farmer's balance sheet in Year C and that in Year D of £20,000 is a fair indication of the Year D loss.

JOHN ENGLAND
BALANCE SHEET

As at 31 March	£	Year A £	£	£	Year B £	£	Year C £	£	£
Fixed assets									
Freeholds		35,000			35,000				35,000
Plant and machinery		6,000			9,000				8,000
Total fixed assets		41,000			44,000				43,000
Current assets									
Debtors	2,000			1,000			20,000		
Stock	27,000			31,000			35,000		
		29,000			32,000			55,000	
Less: Current liabilities									
Creditors	5,000			7,000			6,000		
Bank	50,000			62,000			102,000		
	55,000			69,000			108,000		
Net deficit		26,000			37,000				53,000
Net worth		15,000			7,000				(10,000)
Represented by:									
Private loan		16,000			16,000				16,000
Building society mortgage		10,000			10,000				10,000
Private loan		(11,000)			(19,000)				(36,000)
		15,000			7,000				(10,000)
Sales		50,000			70,000				120,000
Loss		2,000			8,000				17,000
After drawings		3,000			5,500				6,000
Bank account:									
Lowest debit		38,000			41,000				2,000
Highest debit		60,000			90,000				105,000

MOOR FARM, AXTON
CONFIDENTIAL FARMER'S BALANCE SHEET

As at 2 March Year D	Owned	Acreage Tenanted
Arable	29	11 (rent £500 per annum)
Grass	108	
Woodland	2	
Total	139	11

Liabilities	£	Assets	£
Overdraft	33,000	65 dairy cows @ £650	42,250
PAYE	500	32 stores @ £400	12,800
Creditors	2,000	I bull	1,000
		250 ewes @ £50	12,500
		5 rams @ £100	500
	35,500		69,050
Bank loan	98,000	Machinery	12,500
Private loan	16,000	Land and buildings	208,500
Building society mortgage (on cottage)	10,000	Cottage	15,000
	159,500	Life policy surrender value	
Net worth	148,050	(total cover £6,000)	2,500
	307,550		307,550

NOTES
1. The overdraft is charged at 2½% over base rate and the loan at 3% over base rate. The private loan is at 11% fixed for the next five years and the current building society rate is 12%.
2. The cottage is used for 'holiday lets' and produces £2,000 per annum.
3. Assume all valuations of the assets are realistic.
4. The bank has a first mortgage over the land and buildings.
5. Today's balances are: current account £32,500 debit; loan account £97,000 debit.

ACCOUNTING RATIOS

	Year A	Year B	Year C	Year D (confidential farmer's balance sheet)
Net gearing (%)	–	–	–	106
Current ratio	0.53:1	0.46:1	0.51:1	0.51:1
Net profit (before drawings) (%)	2.0	(3.6)	(9.2)	–
Net profit (after drawings) (%)	(6.0)	(11.4)	(14.2)	–

John England is not the sort of farmer to be either willing to or capable of producing an accurate budget. Looking at his rental equivalent, therefore, is an appropriate means of assessing the financial position of the farm enterprise and whether it can be made viable. The rental equivalent is calculated as follows:

RENTAL EQUIVALENT

	£
Overdraft interest (say, av. bal. £31,000)	4,030
Bank loan interest (say, av. bal. £96,000)	12,430
Private loan interest @ 11%	1,760
Building society mortgage @ 12%	1,200
Rent	500
	19,920

The rental equivalent is therefore £133 per acre, which is far too high for England to manage. In its current state the farm enterprise is not viable. If matters are allowed to continue the borrowing will rise, and the security margin, which is currently adequate at 35%, would be eroded to an unjustified extent.

Given the current security position, it is probably not unreasonable to pay the £5,000 cheque in today, but this should be on the understanding that matters will not get any worse and that an investigation of the business is carried out.

England is desperately in need of outside advice, which might come from ADAS, the Milk Marketing Board, or the bank's own farming advisory service. It is likely that any investigation will throw up the need for England to reduce his financial commitments to a more reasonable level. The only way he can do this is for him to sell some of his land.

If he sold, say 60 acres, which would produce around £90,000, plus the cottage at £15,000, he could reduce his borrowing to around £56,000. This would probably consist of the private loan of £16,000, leaving bank borrowing around £40,000. The total annual interest could then be reduced to around £7,500, giving a rental equivalent of around £83 per acre for the remaining 90 acres. While this is still somewhat on the high side, with the benefit of outside expert advice it is hoped that England would have a chance of surviving.

11

Trade finance

Trade finance has always been seen as a specialist business by banks. They recognize this through the establishment of specialist trade finance departments staffed with product specialists, who have all the knowledge of the often complex technicalities of procedure and documentation involved. This book is meant for the generalist lender so this chapter is not going to go in to deep detail about products that are not usually seen by an ordinary domestic lender.

Fundamentally, there are two main types of trade finance transaction:

(a)   export finance;

(b)   import finance.

Export finance

The main ways customers seek payment for exports are:

(a)   *Open account* – Collecting overseas debtors in exactly the same way as for normal domestic transactions.

(b)   *Outward collections* – These can either be 'clean', i.e. secured by an accepted a bill of exchange alone, or 'documentary', a bill of exchange plus the documents of title to the goods being shipped.

Export finance methods do not have to be special. There is no reason why finance should not simply be provided by way of overdraft or by discounting the bills of exchange involved. The borrowing will essentially be a typical working capital facility to finance stock and debtors, albeit that these will be overseas.

Specialist export finance methods are really about retaining a better security position and controlling receipt of debtors more formally. They are therefore not available where payment is on open account terms but are based on the existence of a bill of exchange. There are two main methods of finance:

(a) *Advances against bills held for collection* – This is a lending made against individual bills, or a portfolio of bills held for collection. The primary source of repayment will be payment of the bills by the overseas debtor. Full recourse to the exporter remains in the event the debtor defaults. Security over the debtors can be obtained by taking a letter of hypothecation over them. It should be recognized however that a letter of hypothecation is a relatively weak form of security, and will rank behind any debenture given by the borrower. The goods in the transaction may also be regarded as security but not where the collection is clean or they are released against acceptance of the bill. In such cases the lender loses control of the goods before payment is made.

(b) *Bills negotiated* – A bills negotiated facility differs from an advance made against bills held for collection (AABC) in that, whereas for an AABC facility a set percentage of the value of the bills held is advanced, the lender essentially buys the bills at face value from the exporter, less a discount to cover interest costs. Full recourse to the exporter is retained in the event the bill is dishonoured. Because the lender 'owns' the bill, the security in the debtors is better than for an AABC exposure. The position of stock as security is the same. The downside is that a bills negotiated facility has to be for 100% of the value of the bills rather than a proportion.

For both types of facility, the main lending considerations are the same. The standing of the borrower is paramount because in the event of non-payment by the overseas debtor there is recourse to the borrower. This recourse might occur because the debtor proves to be a poor credit risk or the goods might be rejected on quality or other grounds.

The other main consideration is the quality of the overseas debtors. The factors that influence this are:

(a) Are the debts insured with a reputable insurer?

(b) Is there a good spread of debtors in respect of buyers, amounts and countries?

(c) Are up-to-date status reports held on the debtors?

(d) Has the exchange risk on currency bills been covered forward?

(e) What proportion of the debts might be affected by the imposition of exchange control restrictions in overseas countries with a poor reputation for paying?

(f) Will the underlying goods provide good security for the transaction?

There are other ways of financing exports but these are almost always handled by specialist units within banks because of their complexity and/or the extra risks involved. Only one of these is worthy of mention here, and that is forfaiting.

Forfaiting

Forfaiting works by the forfaiter (usually a bank or other financial institution) purchasing, without recourse to the exporter, bills of exchange or promissory notes representing the payment for goods. The bills are purchased at a discount and the forfaiter then relies entirely on the overseas debtor for repayment. So with forfaiting facilities there is no traditional credit assessment of the exporter although the forfaiter will need to be satisfied that the goods will be of the right quality etc.

The case studies at the end of this chapter do not contain any examples of export finance. This is deliberate, because the basic credit assessment is the same as for any working capital lending, and the principles are well covered in Chapter 3. I have chosen instead to devote more space to the more common and fraught subject for many lenders, import finance with particular emphasis on documentary credits.

Import finance

As with exports, there is no reason why imports should not be paid for on open account. However, many overseas exporters will require more certainty of payment, particularly from businesses that they feel unable to credit-assess themselves. This additional certainty comes in the form of a conditional bank guarantee of payment, usually in the form of a documentary credit.

Documentary credit facilities

A documentary letter of credit represents an obligation on the bank to pay the supplier of goods provided the supplier meets the terms of the credit, including the provision of the documents of title to the goods being shipped. Once an irrevocable letter of credit is in existence, all the overseas supplier has to do is meet its terms and conditions, and the lender has to pay.

The argument is sometimes put forward that documentary credit facilities carry lower risk than simple borrowing. This view is based on the potential availability of the goods being purchased as security. But goods can be regarded as providing security only when:

(a)   The documents of title stipulate release against payment not acceptance.

(b)   The goods will be readily saleable, e.g. commodity products not fashion or specialist goods.

(c)   The documents enable the lender to acquire legal title to the goods. This generally means bills of lading and not airway bills or lorry consignment notes.

(d)   The supplier is of high integrity – the lender will deal only with the documents of title not the actual goods, so it is important that the supplier ships them in the prescribed form.

The fact is that a documentary credit liability eventually produces a debit to the customer's bank account, and where there is an existing overdraft or insufficient credit balance it will produce a borrowing. The credit assessment should be based on this – a contingent liability that will generally turn into a real one.

Avalising

Avalising is another way of a bank's guaranteeing a payment to an overseas exporter. It involves adding the bank's name to a bill or promissory note on behalf of the drawee (the importer). This guarantee, unlike a documentary credit, is unconditional.

As for a documentary credit, the credit assessment should reflect a contingent liability turning into a borrowing.

Exchange risk

Trade transactions may well be denominated in sterling, but a high proportion are denominated in US dollars or other foreign currency. Where this is the case there is a risk that adverse movements in exchange rates may result in less sterling being received or more being paid than originally anticipated.

This risk can be eliminated by hedging, usually using a forward exchange contract, which effectively fixes the exchange rate at the outset of the transaction.

The lender who provides forward contracts incurs two types of risk:

(a) *Settlement risk* – This occurs where the bank pays away currency before reimbursement from the customer; the bank will be on risk for the full amount dispatched, albeit for only a few days.

(b) *Marginal risk* – This arises when a forward contract has to be liquidated resulting in either a profit or a loss, depending on the spot rate at the time of the liquidation. A loss will mean that the customer's liability to the bank is increased by the amount of the loss.

Another way of hedging is by using currency options. The holder of an option has the right, but not the obligation, to buy or sell a specified amount of currency at an agreed rate within a specified period. The granter of an option does not incur a credit risk because the holder does not have to exercise it if the rate is not advantageous.

Case 1

The Famous Brush Company Limited manufactures hair brushes. It was established 70 years ago but has banked with you for only 18 months. You agreed to take over the account when the business was acquired by one of your wealthy customers, John Sullivan, who injected £500,000 into the company when it was in severe financial difficulties. Most of Sullivan's assets are tied up in family trusts, and the £500,000 was provided as a 15-year loan at 10% p.a. from this source.

You have a high regard for Sullivan, who is 53 years old and has been a successful entrepreneur. His particular expertise has been in retail marketing. He saw in Famous Brush a good brand that has been poorly marketed. By using his contacts in the retail trade he was able to boost sales by 33% and return the company to profit for the first time for five years.

The company budgeted sales of £2.6 million and net profit of £375,000 for the current financial year up to the end of March Year D. However, there have been difficulties over the quality of some of the brushes, which has led to their return by retailers. Current estimates are that sales for the year to 31 March Year D will be £2,015,000 and net profit around £50,000.

Famous Brush subcontracts all its manufacturing to suppliers in the Far East. Sullivan had switched some of its work to new suppliers to obtain lower prices. He acknowledges this was a mistake and is now using only the company's original suppliers.

By paying by documentary credit, the company is able to get 90 days' credit from its suppliers. To keep the risk to the company low, Sullivan opens the credits only when he has firm orders from major retailers. The retailers order in the spring for Christmas, and in the autumn for the spring season, so there are two peaks in the demand for documentary credit facilities.

Six months ago your regional office agreed an £800,000 documentary credit facility on the basis that this would be covered either once by cash deposits or one and a half times by debtors. It was also a condition that the family trust loan be postponed to the bank and that, as security, the bank would have a debenture and an unlimited guarantee from Sullivan.

Sullivan is unhappy with the anticipated low profitability for Year D. He has been investigating selling hand mirrors with the company's brand on them, and the retailers have promised orders totalling £600,000 for the spring season. The cost to Famous Brush would be only £400,000, and so the new product would generate £200,000 of additional profit.

To complete the orders, the company will need an additional £400,000 documentary credit facility for the next six months.

FAMOUS BRUSH COMPANY LIMITED
BALANCE SHEETS

As at 31 March	Year A		Year B		Year C	
	£	£	£	£	£	£
Current assets						
Cash	49,645		32,738		375,994	
Debtors	406,863		265,651		434,264	
Stock	32,797	489,305	7,881	306,270	66,169	876,427
Current liabilities						
Creditors	561,705		322,477		606,979	
Hire purchase	13,967		9,234		7,408	
Bank	174,821		416,974		–	
Tax	10,508	(761,001)	10,065	(758,750)	53,554	(667,941)
Net current assets		(271,696)		(452,480)		208,486
Fixed assets						
Motor vehicles	20,627		29,779		28,370	
Fixtures and fittings	11,282	31,909	10,719	40,498	9,114	37,484
		239,787)		(411,982)		245,970
Long-term loans		(1,470)		(35,720)		(474,754)
Net assets (deficit)		(241,257)		(447,702)		(228,784)
Financed by:						
Share capital		10,000		10,000		10,000
Profit and loss account		(251,257)		(457,702)		(238,784)
		(241,257)		(447,702)		(228,784)

PROFIT AND LOSS SUMMARY

12 months to 31 March	Year A £	Year B £	Year C £
Sales	1,602,771	1,527,869	2,029,450
Gross profit	433,265	460,554	584,055
Interest paid	106,807	100,576	66,244
Profit (loss) before tax	(265,226)	(189,419)	215,963

ACCOUNTING RATIOS

	Year A	Year B	Year C
Net gearing (%) (postponed loans as capital)	–	–	Nil
Interest cover (times)	–	–	4.3
Credit given (days)	93	63	78
Credit taken (days)	175	110	153
Stock turnover (days)	10	3	153
Current ratio	0.64:1	0.40:1	1.31:1
Acid test	0.60:1	0.39:1	1.21:1
Gross profit margin (%)	27	30	29
Net profit (loss) margin (%)	(16.5)	(12.4)	10.6

Sullivan is a valuable customer whom the bank would want to help. He has a strong track record, including the turnaround he has already effected at Famous Brush. He is not, however, infallible. The poor quality control in connection with the new suppliers represents a failure of management. But he has recognized the problem and acted to put it right.

Similarly he is not satisfied with the poor anticipated current year performance, and is taking logical steps to improve it. The extension of the product range into a complementary area will enable him to leverage the value of the brand, and also uses his own marketing skills and strong retail contacts. The quality of the mirrors will have to be good. The company cannot afford any more slip-ups if the retail buyers' confidence is to be maintained in their products.

Looking at the financial health of the business, only the most recent balance sheet reflects Sullivan's stewardship of the company. There is a good gross margin on the products so sales performance in volume terms should produce good profits. Sullivan is right to concentrate on sales performance.

The liquidity figures in the year-end balance sheets are probably distorted by the seasonal nature of the business and must be interpreted with care. But the high cash balance at the end of Year C does suggest good credit control in operation.

The business is able to operate without an overdraft but it is only the existence of the bank support through the documentary credits that enables so much credit taken to be obtained. The liquidity position from the bank's point of view is not as good as it looks.

The bank will have to pay if the documents of title are in order. The purchase of goods only against firm orders gives the bank some protection as they will quickly be turned into cash after arrival in the UK. Bu if there was another problem with product quality the bank would be heavily exposed to the retailers' not paying. Even with the trust loan postponed, the company has little fat to fall back on.

It should be possible to extend the existing security formula to the extra facility, as debtors would be 1.5 times the purchase cost of the goods (because of the good profit margin). But the security will be available only if the transactions go according to plan. Security is taken to cover situations when things have gone wrong so this is of limited use. Sullivan's guarantee may be of limited value too as his assets appear to be in family trusts.

The existing facilities are generous and marked on the back of Sullivan's track record. While the risk in the extra requirement is exactly the same as in the old, the size of the amount matters. The bank is being asked to take the same risk as the proprietor for a much lower reward. The additional amount is just too rich. Sullivan could probably come up with more cash to support the business, and this is what he should do.

Case 2

Cover Fashions Limited was established 14 years ago and imports men's and women's raincoats and jackets from China and sells them to retail outlets in the UK.

The company currently banks with a foreign bank in the UK, which is closing its operations in Britain. The business has been introduced to you by that bank.

The company operates from leasehold premises in London. The premises consist of an office, a design studio and a showroom. The stock is held at freight-forwarding warehouses, where it is re-labelled, pressed and prepared for delivery to retailers.

The directors tell you that 98% of goods are pre-sold before orders are placed with the manufacturers in China. The Chinese factories require payment by sight letter of credit.

The garments are designed by the company, and orders are taken following the production of samples in the UK, which are shown to the retailers. 75% of sales are to major UK department stores and retail chains.

The company is family owned. The managing director, Thomas Cover, owns 65% of the shares. He is a chartered accountant in his mid-50s. His son, Richard, is the other main director and joined the company five years ago, having previously worked as a buyer for a large department store group.

The directors wish to continue the facilities they currently enjoy from the foreign bank. These consist of an overdraft and/or documentary credit limit of £1.5 million, together with a complementary £1.5 million forward exchange limit to cover the fact that the Chinese manufacturers require payment in US dollars.

The business is seasonal, with peak selling being in the spring and autumn. The autumn season is the most important, when two thirds of sales occur.

The company does not produce formal budgets or cash flow forecasts, and its present bank has not requested them. The directors have explained to you that forecasting is so dependent on orders received that producing an annual forecast months in advance is pointless.

The present bank have, as security, a debenture giving a fixed and floating charge over company assets and an unlimited guarantee from Thomas Cover supported by a second charge over his house, which had an equity of £450,000 when last valued.

COVER FASHIONS LIMITED
BALANCE SHEETS

As at 31 January	Year A			Year B	
	£	£		£	£
Current assets					
Cash	90,720			126,802	
Debtors	699,719			880,799	
Stock	331,987	1,122,426		359,451	1,367,052
Current liabilities					
Creditors	141,657			77,236	
Bank	12,981			222,944	
Taxation	199,011	(353,649)		113,344	(413,524)
Net current assets		768,777			953,528
Fixed assets					
Leasehold improvements	1,162			871	
Fixtures and fittings	29,509			22,973	
Motor vehicles	27,701	58,732		6,750	30,594
		827,149			984,122
Financed by:					
Share capital		150,000			150,000
Profit and loss account		677,149			834,122
		827,149			984,122

PROFIT AND LOSS SUMMARY

Year to 31 January	Year A	Year B	Year C (Draft)
	£	£	£
Sales	7,091,083	7,063,330	6,966,705
Gross profit	896,231	654,453	710,640
Directors' remuneration	(40,000)	(40,000)	(40,000)
Interest received	6,805	10,646	5,411
Interest paid	(8,522)	(6,217)	(10,632)
Profit before tax	597,542	327,020	356,120
Tax	(198,895)	(90,147)	–
Dividends	(120,250)	(79,900)	–
Retained profit	278,397	156,973	–

ACCOUNTING RATIOS

	Year A	Year B	Year C (Draft)
Net gearing (%)	–	9.8	–
Current ratio	3.17:1	3.31:1	–
Acid test	2.24:1	2.44:1	–
Credit given (days)	36	46	–
Credit taken (days)	8	4	–
Stock turnover (days)	20	20	–
Gross margin (%)	12.6	9.3	10.2
Net margin (%)	8.4	4.6	5.1
Interest cover (times)	71	54	34

This is a well-established business from a plausible source of introduction. Some caution is necessary but the opportunity looks interesting.

By manufacturing in China, the company should be a low-cost producer. Care will be needed over the quality of the garments because, under the terms of the documentary credit, the goods are paid for once the documents are presented. Does the company have the goods inspected in China before shipment?

It is positive that 98% of the goods are pre-sold as this reduces the risk to the business. Moreover, with 75% of sales going to good-quality customers, bad debts should not be a problem.

The management team looks well qualified and experienced. The size of the capital base suggests they have performed well historically.

Given the importance of the autumn season, the balance sheet is probably struck at the best point in the company's liquidity cycle but, even so, the capital structure is good with gearing at a very acceptable level, albeit at the seasonal low point. Potential gearing at 150% is not unreasonable for the short seasonal peaks given the relative certainty of income from firm orders. There is a good record of retentions, with more to come from Year C's performance.

Sales have been flat but the company has done well to improve both gross and net margins in Year C, although these still lag well behind the Year A performance.

The interest charge is low and interest cover is strong – a reflection of the good capital structure. However, interest is not the only finance charge. The documentary credit commission will also be a significant cost.

It is disappointing that there are no formal forecasts because the directors must have some sort of idea of what they want to happen. Without projections it is difficult to know whether the amount being requested is right or not, but the directors have been in the business for many years and with the static pattern of recent sales, it should be sufficient.

As the letters of credit are at sight, the bank's period of risk effectively occurs when the debit hits the bank account and produces borrowing. So the key issue is whether the overdraft thereby created will be repaid from sales.

The debenture should provide good current asset cover at the seasonal peak, given that the good capital base has few fixed assets to finance. But at some points the current assets will mainly be stock rather than debtors and stock in this type of business is generally poor security. The safety of the proposition is heavily reliant on the quality of the goods being sound and the fact that the garments are largely pre-sold.

The directors have a solid track record, and the guarantee and second charge give comfort and are evidence of Cover senior's commitment.

All in all the business looks a good one, which is worth taking on. Ideally the bank should try to impose more discipline by having individual loans for individual transactions, but with the current bank allowing finance on overdraft this may be difficult to achieve.

Case 3

Michael Lancaster and Jeremy York are both in their early 30s. For the past 10 years they have worked for a leading commodity dealing company that buys and sells major commodities such as tea, sugar, cocoa and grain. Lancaster and York have specialized in sugar trading.

About six months ago they left their employer to set up a new company called Lancaster-York Commodities Limited. A wealthy individual, who knew their expertise well, provided the new company with its initial share capital of £500,000. Of this sum, £50,000 has been invested in acquiring leasehold premises and the office equipment etc. needed to trade sugar.

The company's bank account was opened at your branch, as both York and Lancaster had maintained satisfactory personal accounts with you for a number of years. The account has operated entirely in credit, moving up and down between £450,000 and £100,000 as purchases and sales of bulk sugar have taken place. The present balance on the account is £200,000.

The two directors call to see you. They tell you that, in their first six months' trading, they have carried out 10 successful deals, and even after taking start-up costs into account the company has made a profit of £35,000. They now wish to undertake some bigger transactions, which will require an element of bank funding.

The first of these is described as follows:

(a)   Lancaster-York wishes to purchase 1,250 tonnes of raw sugar from a grower in Trinidad at £420 per tonne – total cost £525,000 to be paid up front.

(b)   It has negotiated a contract to sell the sugar to a major French sugar refiner, to be paid for on delivery at Marseilles in France, subject to inspection, at a price of £460 per tonne.

(c)   The sugar is part of Trinidad's European Union (EU) quota and, subject to meeting minimum quality standards, the EU Intervention Board is committed to buying it at a minimum price of £450 per tonne.

(d)   Shipment, insurance and other direct costs will amount to £20 per tonne.

(e)   From shipment to delivery, the transaction is likely to take 25 days to complete.

(f)   Lancaster-York requires a produce loan from the bank of £400,000 for up to six weeks to help finance the transaction.

This is a relatively new business so caution is necessary. But Lancaster and York have a considerable amount of experience of the sugar trading business to draw on, and the fact that someone who knows them is prepared to back them to the extent of £500,000 is impressive.

The initial trading has been cautious, with all deals self-financed. It would be helpful to have some details of the past deals to see how the proposed one compares. Management accounts should be seen to confirm their profitability.

The capital base of the company is strong – now £535,000 – so overall gearing should be reasonable. The current bank balance indicates that there are some other small deals currently under way, and details of these should be obtained, including a short-term cash flow forecast which will give an indication of potential alternative sources of repayment should the proposed proposition go wrong. An agreement to lend for this deal is unlikely to be a 'one off' so the parameters set should recognize this.

The deal apparently generates a good profit:

	£
Cost of sugar	525,000
Shipment etc.	25,000
	550,000
Income	575,000
Profit	25,000

(before interest, overheads, etc.)

And there is a good fallback position, in that the sugar could be sold at the EU intervention price – this would produce income of £562,500.

There is therefore a good margin in the transaction for the bank – lending £400,000 against semi-guaranteed income of at least £562,500. So what are the risks? Essentially they fall into four areas:

(a) *Exchange risk* – The sugar is being paid for in French francs, so if a guaranteed sterling profit is to be achieved, forward cover must be put in place.

(b) *Physical delivery* – Will the supplier deliver the sugar for shipment? Ideally the company should pay only on evidence of shipment. The bank should check on the integrity of the supplier. There is also a risk that the sugar could be lost during shipment, but this can be covered by insurance.

(c) *Quality* – The quality of the sugar is an issue. It must be of sufficient quality when shipped, and then must not deteriorate during shipment. Ideally it should be inspected before being shipped, and an experienced shipping company should be used.

(d) *Control* – The bank must keep control of the sugar until payment is received. A letter of pledge over the goods should be taken, and the bank should use its correspondent bank in Trinidad to obtain possession of the shipping documents when payment is made to the supplier. On arrival in Marseilles, the goods should be warehoused in the bank's name. This runs the risk of demurrage costs having to be paid by the bank if the goods are not released quickly to the French buyer. Documents of title will have to be delivered to the buyer on trust to allow the quality inspection to take place, so the bank will need to be completely satisfied as to both the integrity and the creditworthiness of the buyer.

The detailed control of the sugar is crucial to the success of the transaction, but provided the right controls are in place the risk looks acceptable.

12

Acquisition finance

Acquisition finance is a generic term that can be applied to any lending advanced to aid the purchase of a business. More specifically it is a term that is in general use to describe the financing of management buy-outs (MBOs) and management buy-ins (MBIs). It is in this latter context that it is used for the purposes of this chapter (although many of the concepts used to assess the validity of an MBO or MBI lending proposition can equally be applied to other types of business purchase – e.g. whether the proposed purchase price represents good value or not).

An MBO is the sale by the shareholders of an existing business to the existing management team. An MBI is the sale of an existing business to a new incoming management team. In both cases, the transaction is usually facilitated by a venture capital house's putting up part of the funding need. The typical outcome is an exchange of the current owners' equity interest for a large element of debt. This, in conjunction with any goodwill element payable, leads to high – often very high – initial gearing. Getting a safe funding structure in place, which meets the needs of the acquiring management, the venture capital house and the debt provider, is crucial.

Structuring the financing

The main components of MBO/MBI funding are as follows:

(a) *Ordinary shares* – These give the shareholders economic ownership of the company. In the context of an MBO/MBI it is only the holders of ordinary shares who benefit from the increased capital value of the business through capital gains. So the ordinary shares will be split between the financing parties. The lion's share will go to the management, but the venture capital house will usually have a significant percentage, and any mezzanine lender (see below) may also have a small percentage. The main driver of the split will be the relative power of the parties. The venture capital house will have a forecast rate of return based on its assessment of the likely future performance of the business, and this will have to meet its requirement before it will invest. However, if there is significant competition from other venture capital houses to win the mandate, then the management's hand will be strengthened.

(b) *Preference shares* – A preference share is basically a priority share. It is entitled to a dividend before ordinary shareholders, and in the event of a winding-up the preference shareholders would be paid before the ordinary shareholders. Dividends on preference shares are usually of a fixed nature. Preference shareholders do not usually have voting rights. Venture capital houses tend to invest a significant portion of their funding in the form of preference shares. This enables the management team to qualify for a larger share of economic ownership than would be the case if all the funds were provided by ordinary shares.

(c) *Mezzanine debt* – Mezzanine debt tends to be a loan secured on the assets of the business behind the bank's senior debt, and usually has the benefit of an 'equity kicker'. The equity kicker usually takes the form of a warrant that entitles the mezzanine lender to buy a small percentage of the business (typically 5%) for a nominal price. Interest on the mezzanine debt is often set at one or two percent higher than the senior debt rate.

(d) *Senior debt* – This is the term given to the bank loans and other lines of credit such as overdrafts for working capital, and is so named in recognition of the bank's place in the financial pecking order: that is to say, the bank has first call on cash flow to service the debt due to it and normally first call on any security. Typically senior debt takes the form of a medium-term loan, repayable over a period of up to seven years, plus a working capital overdraft.

Rationale for the structure

The first driver for the structure would appear to be the price to be paid for the business, but in practice it is often the financing structure that determines the price. The deal will be viable only if all the financiers of different persuasions and risk and reward appetites are comfortable with their relative positions.

The financial model of the deal must enable the equity investors to get their target returns and the mezzanine debt and senior debt to be serviced over a reasonable period. An MBO/MBI is dependent on the amount of the cash flows the business can generate, and so the value of the business will be restricted to the amount of finance the company can service.

What then is the appropriate split between the different types of funding?

In other words, what level of gearing is required to give the necessary return on capital to the investors while also producing a satisfactory risk for the lenders?

In practice, gearing levels are proposed by the deal arranger/structurer. The arranger is usually an accountant or the venture capital house itself. The first step is to get the management to propose a business plan. Then the arranger will produce a financial model around it. This will drive out the appropriate returns required by the venture capital house based on assumptions for debt servicing that the arranger believes will be acceptable to a lender.

The structure is then passed to the bank, which will look at the prospects for repayment with a critical eye based on sensitivity analysis and subject to confirmation of the validity of assumptions through due diligence to be carried out by independent accountants.

If the structure is not acceptable to the bank and no alternative lender can be found, then it will have to be amended. The probable knock-on effect of this will be that the price will have to be reduced because no more equity will be put in if the venture capital house is to achieve its target return. Very often there is an alternative lender in the form of the seller of the business. Rather than take a reduction in the price being obtained, the seller may be prepared to lend the shortfall to the purchaser in the form of what are known as vendor loan notes. The bank will usually want to see such loan notes subordinated in terms of both balance sheet ranking and repayment.

Senior debt capacity

This is the key element for the lending banker. There is no magic mathematical formula to be applied because as for all businesses the repayment capacity will vary from company to company based on many different factors. Different sectors have different characteristics, and will be affected differently by factors such as the economic cycle.

The analysis will usually take two parts:

(a)   cash flow analysis – the debt service relationship;

(b)   the value of secondary exits.

Cash flow analysis – the debt service relationship

The business plan and the financial model derived from it will contain a view of future cash flows that can be tested as part of the due diligence process. In particular, a close look should be taken at the underlying assumptions to ensure they are valid in the new circumstances in which the business will be operating. For example, the management team may not be able to obtain the same terms of trade as an independent business as were available to the business when it was part of a larger group.

Sensitivity analysis must be undertaken to establish the impact on the projections of slippage (and/or exceptionally good performance) on the ability to generate cash. Sensitivities will usually be based on the analysis of a number of key variables. The following list is not exhaustive but contains the main elements:

(a)   the impact of the loss of an important customer;

(b)   the effects of increasing competition on gross margin;

(c)   the effects of reduced growth or slippage in the forecasts;

(d)   the impact of changes in terms of trade available;

(e)   the extent to which planned capital expenditure is essential or could be deferred in extremis.

Having considered all of these factors, the lender needs to look at how well the business is able to service its financial obligations under a variety of different scenarios. It will be appreciated that the best-laid plans will sometimes go wrong, and some margin for error must be available. The lender will usually require a debt/service covenant that builds in a surplus to cover this margin for error.

If the sensitivity analysis throws up reasonable scenarios that produce extreme cash flow variations, then the deal may not work at all. MBOs/MBIs almost inevitably involve high capital gearing when looked at from a traditionally cautious banking point of view. So certainty of repayment to rapidly reduce the risks associated with high gearing is essential. Stability and dependability in the future cash flows must be present.

At this juncture it is worth making a point not generally appreciated by lenders not used to dealing with this type of transaction. It is to do with the assessment of gearing. Venture capitalists tend to talk about gearing as being the relationship between debt funding and shareholders' investment. In other words, they do not deduct goodwill from the shareholders' funds in the balance sheet as traditional bankers have been taught to do to ensure a prudent approach. For this type of transaction the venture capitalists' standpoint has to be accepted if the bankers are to participate in the acquisition finance business (and, of course, some banks may consider the risks of this type of transaction to be too high – although history shows credit losses are very similar to 'ordinary' lending). The reason is straightforward and comes out of a statement made above. If the value of a business is equivalent to the amount of funding that can be raised to buy it, and businesses with the most dependable cash flows can raise the highest debt funding, then it almost inevitably follows that the goodwill element in the best transactions will be very high relative to shareholders' funding. Indeed experience suggests that businesses with good future cash flow certainty almost always have an initial negative net tangible asset position. In fact the presence of an apparently strongly positive net tangible asset position may be a reason for caution because it indicates that a relatively low price is being paid for the business, which may reflect inside knowledge of potential cash flow instability. Traditional bankers are not used to this type of thinking, but it has to be taken on board.

The value of secondary exits

Deals will go wrong. History has taught bankers that even the best sensitivity and scenario analysis does not protect lenders against the impact of external shocks etc. that were not foreseen. So the bank will want some alternative secondary source of repayment to be available.

Secondary exits are traditionally linked to the value of the forced sale of security, and debentures and other charges over assets are normal. The problem with this approach is that it may ignore the cash flow value of the business. A high proportion of MBOs/MBIs that go wrong get reconstructed to reduce the cash outflow burden to one that the business can sustain. A new value is put on the business, which can then find new owners as a going concern. So looking at the possible disposal value of the business is something that the bank should consider, perhaps with the help of the independent accountants undertaking the due diligence process.

In practice, the venture capital house will stand to lose more than the bank from a winding-up, and so there is a highly motivated party with good connections to assist in the orderly disposal or refinancing of the business to the benefit of everyone concerned (with the possible exception of the management team, who, having failed, may be ditched).

Management stake

There is often more heat than light talked about what is an appropriate minimum stake that the management team should have in an MBO/MBI. Ordinary managers in businesses, usually in middle age with heavy family commitments, are not typically possessed of large amounts of spare capital to put into a project. Looking for large sums from them is therefore unrealistic, however unpalatable this may seem when comparing their and the bank's relative risk and reward profiles.

This issue is best considered in the light of the underlying fundamental realities. The most important of these is that the amount of capital provided by most management teams is actually insignificant when compared with the overall financing needs of a typical MBO/MBI. The venture capital house or the bank could usually provide the extra funding being provided by management without much difficulty or changing their own risk/reward equation. So there is a case for saying that the insistence on a management investment is unnecessary.

However, the existence of a quality management team and its commitment to the business going forward will always be fundamental to any deal. The management team must be locked in, and should not be able to walk away without personal penalty if the going starts to get tough. This is the real reason why a management stake is needed. It should be significant in terms of the individual's own resources so that it provides a motivator if the possibility of its loss was to arise.

Case 1

···

Diesel Machinery Limited is currently a wholly owned subsidiary of Conglomerate plc, a large diversified industrial group. Conglomerate plc is in financial difficulties and needs to reduce gearing. It has therefore decided to divest itself of some of its non-core subsidiaries, including Diesel Machinery Limited.

Diesel Machinery Limited was formed 18 years ago as a distributor of diesel engines made by major manufacturers. Its main market (80% of new equipment) is the sale of engines as electricity generating sets, mainly used to provide emergency and standby electrical power. The remainder of sales are to meet specific customer needs; the company adapts engines for installation into customer products.

Two of Diesel's directors, Ian Foster (aged 46), the managing director, and Trevor O'Neill (aged 38), the marketing director, have expressed interest in leading a management buy-out of the company. Both Foster and O'Neill have been in the engineering industry all their working lives, and have worked for Diesel for five and four years respectively. They have been given a great deal of autonomy in running the company but believe it has been under-resourced by Conglomerate plc. They also believe the business could be run more tightly, and have identified ways of reducing overheads by 7%.

Conglomerate has put an asking price of £2.5 million on the business, but Foster and O'Neill believe they can knock this down to £2.2 million and have produced financial projections based on this sum. By re-mortgaging their houses they can, between them, raise £125,000, which will purchase part of the equity of the company. They have found a venture capital house that is prepared to invest the balance in return for £250,000 of the equity and £1,825,000 of redeemable preference shares, provided that a bank can be found to provide initial overdraft facilities of £800,000.

The venture capital house has sent you a copy of the financial projections, as Diesel's offices are near your branch. You are asked whether you are interested in providing the required overdraft.

DIESEL MACHINERY LIMITED

HISTORICAL AND PROJECTED FINANCIAL INFORMATION

	Actuals			Projections		
Year to 30 April	Year A £000	Year B £000	Year C £000	Year D £000	Year E £000	Year F £000
Turnover	7,574	6,271	8,801	9.923	10,901	12,169
Gross profit	1,716	1,446	1,642	2,141	2,409	2,812
Profit before interest and tax	242	125	150	481	595	777
Retained profit	18	(181)	(97)	86	151	276

ACCOUNTING RATIOS

	Year A	Year B	Year C	Year D	Year E	Year F
Gross margin (%)	22.7	23.1	18.7	21.6	22.1	23.1
Net margin (%)	–	–	–4.4	4.9	5.6	
Net gearing (%)	–	–	31	55	61	88
Current ratio	–	–	1.61:1	1.46:1	1.41:1	1.32:1
Acid test	–	–	0.84:1	0.87:1	0.83:1	0.77:1
Credit given (days)	–	–	72	83	79	75
Stock turnover (days)	–	–	67	57	55	54

SALES PROJECTIONS

Year ending 30 April	Year D £000	Year E £000	Year F £000
New equipment	5,348	5,865	6,547
Parts	3,364	3,706	4,137
Servicing	1,211	1,330	1,485
	9,923	10,901	12,169

DIESEL MACHINERY LIMITED
BALANCE SHEET

As at 30 April Opening position £000		Year D £000	Projections Year E £000	Year F £000
	Fixed assets			
147	Plant and machinery	103	59	23
	Current assets			
1,611	Stock	1,557	1,646	1,788
1,746	Debtors	2,257	2,369	2,513
3,357		3,814	4,015	4,301
	Current liabilities			
1,519	Creditors	1,777	1,947	2,144
422	Bank	698	727	905
10	Lease finance	8	7	5
132	Taxation	126	160	213
(2083)		(2,609)	(2,841)	(3,267)
1,274	Net current assets	1,204	1,174	1,036
(21)	Deferred tax	(21)	(21)	(21)
1,400	Net assets	1,286	1,212	1,038
	Financed by:			
375	Share capital	375	375	375
1,825	Preference shares	1,625	1,400	950
(800)	Revenue reserves	(714)	(563)	(287)
1,400		1,286	1,212	1.038

Some of the figures in these financial statements have been subject to rounding.

DIESEL MACHINERY LIMITED
PROJECTED CASH FLOW STATEMENT

Year ending 30 April	Year D £000	Year E £000	Year F £000
Profit before tax	432	531	684
Depreciation	64	64	56
	496	595	740
Working capital changes Increase/ (decrease):			
Stock	54	(89)	(143)
Debtors	(511)	(112)	(144)
Creditors	258	170	198
	(199)	(31)	(90)
Other fund movements:			
Taxation	(150)	(143)	(175)
Dividends paid	(203)	(203)	(180)
Capital expenditure	(20)	(20)	(20)
Preference share redemption	(200)	(225)	(450)
	(572)	(591)	(825)
Net cash flow	(274)	(27)	(175)
Represented by movements in:			
Lease finance	2	2	2
Overdraft	(276)	(29)	(178)
	(274)	(27)	(176)

Some of the figures in these financial statements have been subject to rounding.

This case represents a simple MBO.

The fact that the bank does not know any of the principals involved is not unusual for an MBO, but the venture capital house would usually introduce the business to one of its regular bank contacts, so some caution is needed.

However, the size of the venture capital investment compared with the bank requirement is impressive.

The management's own commitment is significant in terms of their own resources. They should know the business well. Having said this, it has not performed well under their stewardship in the past. Moreover, if it has been under-resourced when part of a major group, then it is unlikely that the new owners will be able to address this issue quickly.

The main product is at the 'heavy' end of the engineering range, and a large portion of new equipment sales are likely to be dependent on the construction market, which tends to be cyclical. This is less than ideal in the context of an MBO, where solid predictable cash flows are needed to reduce borrowing quickly. However, the parts/service element of sales should provide a more stable element of cash flow, and this represents 46% of forecast sales.

What is the attitude of the company's suppliers going to be in the face of their weakened credit covenant? The attitude of the engine supplier will be especially crucial, and needs to be determined.

Looking at the financial analysis, the historical track record of losses has to be a concern. However, it is profitability at the PBIT line that is the most important, given that the interest charge will be different in the new scenario and the business has been profitable at this level.

The projected sales performance looks demanding compared with the recent past. While the new equipment sales forecast might be explained by a cyclical upturn, the increase in parts/service sales probably requires the business to achieve an increase in market share. Why should this be possible?

The gross margin projections are in line with previous performance with the exception of the most recent year, so they should be achievable. The problem comes when gross margin and sales performance are linked. Sales increased in Year C, but this was only on the back of a gross margin reduction, and this does not augur well for the attainment of the future combined sales/gross margin targets.

Gearing looks acceptable going forward, but there has to be an issue in the fact that it increases as the preference shares are redeemed. In fact the venture capital house gets repaid quicker than the bank despite being nominally subordinate. It seems likely that the bank requirement will rise further in the years beyond the forecasts as a result of this process.

Capital expenditure is low compared with the depreciation charge, suggesting a potential short-term cash gain at the expense of a higher cash need in future.

The forecast assumptions look questionable in a number of areas, and thorough due diligence will be required to validate them.

The security position is apparently strong, as the debenture provides excellent debtor cover – over three times in the first two years. However, reservation of title could be a problem. Normally it is difficult to trace title through to debtors, but in this instance it may be possible because the engines are likely to have individual serial numbers. Having said this, the parts/service debtors are significant, and will not be affected by reservation of title.

In favour of the proposition is the relatively low borrowing requirement and good security cover. Against is the preferential exit by the venture capital house (although it should be possible to renegotiate this) and, more importantly, the questions over the forecasts. Due diligence is going to be crucial but if it is positive most banks would lend.

Case 2

Northern Casting Company is a division of a small public engineering company called Engineering Conglomerate plc. Two months ago, Engineering Conglomerate was placed into administrative receivership by its bank. The receiver, who is a partner from one of the major UK accounting firms, has kept the manufacturing businesses that make up Engineering Conglomerate trading while he tries to find buyers for them.

Northern Casting produces high-quality metal components, which are used in the brewing, machine tool, automotive and defence industries. It has a broad spread of customers, no one of which represents more than 5% of sales.

The works manager of Northern Casting, Peter Collins (48), calls to see you. He has maintained a satisfactory personal account with your bank for 20 years. With the help of some of the employees, he wants to purchase the business of Northern Casting Company. He tells you the following:

(a)   The proposed new shareholders can raise £180,000 to invest in the venture.

(b)   A price of £280,000 has been agreed with the receiver for the plant and stock of the business.

(c)   The plant and machinery comprises machine tools, foundry and finishing equipment, which are currently under-utilised. The previous book value of the plant was £250,000.

(d)   The receiver has sold the factory premises occupied by the business separately to a property company. The property company will grant the new venture a 15-year lease subject to five-yearly reviews at an initial rent of £120,000 per annum. However, because the new venture is unproven, the property company is insisting that a bank guarantees the payment of the rent for the first three years.

(e)   The venture will be incorporated into a new limited company and be called Northern Casting Company Limited.

(f)   The receiver has carried out an analysis of the old Northern Casting Company Division accounts over the past three years, and this has been provided to Collins, who has also produced projections for the new venture with the help of an accountant friend.

(g)   There is a requirement for bank support as follows:

Overdraft   £300,000

Loan   £100,000 (5 years, including one year repayment holiday)

Rent guarantee

Collins asks whether you can assist.

NORTHERN CASTING COMPANY
PROFIT AND LOSS SUMMARY

12 months	Actual			Forecast		
	Year A £000	Year B £000	Year C £000	Year 1 £000	Year 2 £000	Year 3 £000
Sales	1,454	1,510	1,219	1,650	1,800	2,000
Cost of sales						
Materials and subcontracting	(475)	(545)	(438)	(578)	(630)	(700)
Labour	(324)	(300)	(261)	(276)	(302)	(335)
Gross profit	655	665	520	796	868	965
Expenses	(489)	(435)	(390)	(622)	(629)	(631)
Profit before tax	166	230	130	174	239	334
After:						
Rent	–	–	–	120	120	120
Depreciation	27	27	24	16	16	16
Director's remuneration	–	–	–	30	30	30
Interest paid	–	–	–	35	26	4

FORECAST BALANCE SHEETS

	Opening position £000	Q1 £000	Q2 £000	Year 1 Q3 £000	Q4 £000	Year 2 £000	Year 3 £000
Current assets							
Cash	–	–	–	–	–	83	313
Debtors	–	344	357	370	383	397	441
Stock	130	130	130	130	130	130	130
	130	474	487	500	513	610	884
Current liabilities							
Trade creditors	–	–	30	62	64	66	73
Bank overdraft	–	275	213	142	9	–	–
VAT payable	–	12	12	13	14	14	15
Accruals	–	21	22	23	24	24	24
Tax	–	8	18	30	43	60	84
	–	(316)	(295)	(270)	(237)	(164)	(196)
Net current assets	130	158	192	230	276	446	688
Bank loan	(100)	(100)	(100)	(100)	(100)	(75)	(50)
Fixed assets							
Plant and machinery	150	146	142	139	134	119	103
Net assets	180	204	234	269	310	490	741
Financed by:							
Share capital	180	180	180	180	180	180	180
Profit and loss	–	24	54	89	130	130	561
	180	204	234	269	310	490	741

ACCOUNTING RATIOS

	Year A	Year B	Year C	Opening Position	Year 1	Forecast Year 2	Year 3
Net gearing (%)	–	–	–	55.6	61.9	–	–
Current ratio	–	–	–	–	-2.16:1	3.72:1	4.51:1
Acid test	–	–	–	–	-1.62:1	2.93:1	3.85:1
Credit given (days)	–	–	–	–	85	81	80
Credit taken (days)	–	–	–	–	40	38	38
Stock turnover (days)	–	– –		–	-56	51	46
Gross margin (%)	45.0	44.0	42.7	–	48,2	48.2	48.2
Net margin (%)	11.4	15.2	10.7	–	10.5	13.3	16.7
Interest cover (times)	–	–	–	–	-6.0	10.2	84.5

This case represents a simple MBO with no venture capital house involvement.

Collins has been a valued personal customer, and the bank would want to be positive if possible. The proposed investment of £180,000 looks quite substantial in terms of Collins's and the workforce's resources.

The shareholding structure will be important given the diverse ownership. It is possible that control of the business could be in too many hands, and there might be insufficient certainty of direction.

The composition of the management team will be a key issue. Collins should understand the production side, but who is going to look after marketing and sales? The finance function appears light. Collins had to use a 'friend' to produce the forecasts, which suggests that there is no one within the business itself, and this must be a concern.

The price being paid for the business looks fair given the book value of the plant. On a P/E basis the price looks cheap at just over two times last year's profits.

Buying just the plant and stock avoids the risks involved in buying the business as a whole, such as hidden bad debts etc. It is possible that customer confidence has been damaged by the receivership, so it would be helpful to understand the strength of the current order book.

The financial analysis is complicated by the absence of audited accounts. The business was previously only a division of Engineering Conglomerate. Some sort of warranty covering the accuracy of the historical figures should be sought from the receiver.

Historic profitability has been good, with net margin always above 10%. There is a problem though, because the historic figures do not contain a full set of overheads. In future the business will be carrying additional costs for rent, interest etc., which are at a level in the first forecast year that would have wiped out the last historic year's profit.

The profit forecast for next year is predicated on a substantial increase in sales. Having said this, sales last year were well down on the previous year, perhaps because of the effects of the receivership – the reason needs to be established. It might be possible to achieve the sales volume, but the forecasts also assume a much higher gross margin than has been achieved before.

The overheads look conservative, but there have to be question marks over some other figures:

(a) The constant stock figure while sales rise sharply looks wrong.

(b) Will there really be no capital expenditure?

(c) Why can no trade credit be obtained initially but be available later?

As security the bank should be able to take a debenture. What would this be worth?

		£
Debtors @ 70% x £344,000	=	240,800
Stock @ 10% x £130,000	=	13,000
Plant @ 25% x £146,000	=	36,500
		290,300

To cover the peak borrowing of £375,000 plus the rent guarantee. This looks thin. Directors' guarantees would help, but these might be difficult to obtain given the diverse ownership structure.

Overall the proposition looks too naïve. It is difficult to feel confidence in the management or its plans. Security cover is also thin. The deal should be declined.

Case 3

Advanced Products Limited was established 30 years ago, and manufactures high-specification components for the motor industry. For the last 10 years the company has been part of a medium-size industrial group with interests in a number of areas, including plastics and building materials. In recent years Advanced Products has performed poorly despite changes in management and substantial capital expenditure to acquire the latest plant and machinery. Its parent has decided to dispose of the business, and is looking for a buyer.

You have contacts with a firm of venture capitalists, and they have approached you to see if your bank is interested in participating in the financing of a management buy-in of Advanced Products Limited. The proposed structure of the transaction is:

Finance required	*£000*
Acquisition price	2,470
Working capital	400
Deal costs	175
	3,075
Funded by	
Deferred consideration	350
Overdraft	500
Medium Term Loan	900
Management shareholding	40
Investor shareholding	1,255
	3,045

The requirement from the bank is the overdraft and five-year medium-term loan.

The main elements of the proposal are:

(a) The MBI will be undertaken by a William Wallace (age 41), who will operate as managing director on a full-time basis. A new finance director – someone known to Wallace – will also be appointed. Wallace is a graduate engineer and qualified accountant who has been known to the venture capital house for some years. He has a track record as a 'company doctor' in making underperforming engineering companies profitable. He has been looking to acquire a business 'of his own' for two years, and has identified Advanced Products as a good opportunity.

(b) Wallace has had full access to the company and its staff for the past three months. He has had the opportunity of examining internal financial information, and has met all the major suppliers and customers.

(c) Quality control has been a problem, and caused the loss of two major customers in the last financial year. Wallace has discussed the possibility of getting this business back with the companies concerned, and believes they will return when he is in charge.

(d) Wallace has drawn up projections for the future. These, together with the recent trading performance and opening balance sheet position, are to be the subject of due diligence by a national firm of accountants on behalf of the venture capitalists.

(e) An experienced industrialist is to be appointed as non-executive chairman to represent the interests of the outside investors.

(f) The preference shares are redeemable from Year G onwards.

(g) The bank is offered a debenture giving a fixed and floating charge over the company's assets.

ADVANCED PRODUCTS LIMITED
BALANCE SHEET PROJECTIONS

	Opening (£000s)	Year D (£000s)	Year E (£000s)	Year F (£000s)
Fixed assets				
Plant, machinery & vehicles	2,314	1,952	1,681	1,484
Stock	700	914	986	1,086
Debtors	1,228	1,495	1,688	1,938
Creditors	(911)	(1,015)	(1,133)	(1,283)
Dividends	–	(60)	(60)	(60)
Tax	–	(79)	(179)	(328)
Bank balance	77	195	297	691
Working Capital	1,094	1,450	1,599	2,044
Deferred tax	–	(14)	(17)	(16)
Medium-term loan	(900)	(800)	(600)	(400)
Leasing creditor	(863)	(786)	(695)	(686)
Deferred consideration	(350)	(350)	(175)	–
Net Assets	1,295	1,452	1,793	2,426
Financed by:				
Management equity	40	40	40	40
Institutional equity	60	60	60	60
Institutional cumulative				
redeemable preference shares	1,195	1,195	1,195	1,195
Profit and loss	–	157	498	1,131
	1,295	1,452	1,793	2,426

ADVANCED PRODUCTS LIMITED
PROFIT AND LOSS SUMMARY

12 months to 31 December	Actual Year A (£000s)	Year B (£000s)	Year C (£000s)	3 months to 31 March Year D (£000s)	Budget Year D (£000s)	Year E (£000s)	Year F (£000s)
Sales	5,861	5,740	3,673	1,222	5,600	6,700	7,900
Gross profit	1,371	1,784	1,067	501	2,510	3,014	3,589
Overheads including:	2,598	3,373	3,065	551	2,030	2,270	2,470
Depreciation	307	540	676	147	623	600	533
Repairs under warranty	–	82	45	3	13	13	13
Bad debts	63	46	32	6	25	25	25
Group management charge	88	98	72	15	–	–	-
Salaries (including directors' remuneration)	1,114	1,306	1,123	221	830	990	1,060
Redundancy costs	153	157	49	3	–	–	-
Stock provisions	11	123	350	3	–	–	-
Profit before interest and tax	(1,227)	(1,589)	(1,998)	(50)	480	744	1,119
Interest	316	95	121	24	217	214	184
Profit before tax	(1,543)	(1,684)	(2,119)	(74)	263	530	935
TAX	–	–	–	–	46	129	242
Dividends	–	–	–	–	60	60	60
Retained profit	(1,543)	(1,684)	(2,119)	(74)	157	341	633

ACCOUNTING RATIOS

	Year A	Year B	Year C	3 months to 31 Mar Year D	Opening balance sheet	Year D	Year E	Year F
Net gearing (%)	–	–	–	–	130	96	56	16
Current ratio	–	–	–	–	2.2:1	2.3:1	2.2:1	2.2:1
Acid test	–	–	–	–	1.4:1	1.5:1	1.4:1	1.6:1
Credit given (days)	–	–	–	–	–	97	92	90
Credit taken (days)	–	–	–	–	–	189	176	169
Stock turnover (days)	–	–	–	–	–	112	98	92
Gross margin %	23	31	29	41	–	45	45	45
Net margin %	(26.3)	(29.3)	(57.7)	(6.1)	–	4.7	7.9	11.8
Interest cover (times)	–	–	–	–	–	2.2	3.5	6.1

This is an example of a Management Buy-in (MBI). MBIs generally are more risky than MBOs because the management of the business is brand new on top of everything else, and they do not have the sort of detailed knowledge of the business that an existing team brings.

The introduction is from a good source and so needs to be taken seriously. The venture capitalists will be persuading investors to take a higher risk than the bank, and their reputation will be on the line. Their willingness to support Wallace is positive. Even so, the bank still needs to have other references on him, particularly in relation to his previous performance as a company doctor.

The fact that there is going to be a non-executive chairman, who will provide an ongoing independent influence on the business, will be in the bank's interest as well as the investors'.

Wallace's time spent in the business will have given him a good picture of it, and he is committing £40,000 of his own money. However, he cannot have that in-depth knowledge that actually being responsible for the business brings. The existing management team and workforce have been associated with failure, and will have to be motivated to turn things around, which may not be easy. This could be particularly crucial in relation to the critical quality problems the company has been facing. Plant and equipment should be up to date, and little capital expenditure should be needed.

The purchase price at £2,470,000 for net assets of £1,295,000 looks high, particularly for a loss-making business. There has to be an underlying strong assumption that the forecast profits can be achieved to justify the price.

The initial gearing looks high but is probably acceptable in view of the medium-term element. The overdraft is not used at the opening or year-ends in the projections, so a monthly cash flow is needed to justify the request.

The three-year gap before the preference shares start to be redeemed seems reasonable. It would be helpful to see audited accounts for the historical business to put the projections into context. The forecasts indicate that the business should be very liquid, but this is dependent on the high level of projected credit taken, which requires confirmation. Moreover, the profit projections look very ambitious when compared with past performance. A substantial improvement in sales is required. Much will depend on Wallace's winning back the lost business.

Additionally, a much higher gross margin than has been achieved historically is required. and although the first quarter's figures show some improvement in gross profit percentage, even this is not enough. The substantial cut in overheads that has been assumed looks ambitious too, although again there are signs in the first quarter that an improvement can be made.

There do not seem to be any on-off costs for redundancies, despite the fact that a significant cut in salaries is projected. The reduced stock and warranty provisions will need quality improvements if they are to achieved.

The debenture picks up good current asset cover for the bank. Two times cover is available, including one and a half times by debtors. Given the low bad debt record, this should be adequate security. On top of this, there may be some value in the plant and equipment not covered by HP. Chattel mortgages would be needed.

Given the tightness in the projections, an interest cap or hedge for the borrowing should be considered.

This is a difficult decision. Although Wallace has the right background and there is acceptable security cover, the achievement of the projections looks very demanding. The bank could commission its own due diligence but, in the end, due diligence is still only a rather more informed opinion.

Overall it would be better if the proposition was re-engineered through the negotiation of a lower purchase price or a greater proportion of venture capital money compared with bank debt.

Case 4

....

TNC Limited operates a chain of shops selling confectionery, tobacco, newspapers, gifts and toys. The shops are all on short leaseholds and are mainly situated in town centres. The company has a central warehouse and buying organization through which it supplies the shops. Its main competitors are owner-managed, single-shop operations.

The company was founded 35 years ago but was sold last year to Andrew Goode and his family, who are now its directors. Goode is 50 years old and has a background of working in major retailing groups.

Goode believes that the future of the business lies in supplying a wider range of products than currently. This wider range can only be offered in the company's larger shops. He has closed eight of the smaller outlets, and has plans to replace them with new larger stores, which will also sell items such as toiletries.

The Goode family has injected £100,000 into the company since its acquisition, and has reached agreement with a venture capital company which is prepared to invest £500,000 immediately in the form of ordinary shares and a further £400,000 in two years' time in the form of loan stock to help fund the expansion programme. The loan stock will be repayable over five years from the end of Year F and will be secured by a fixed and floating charge over the company's assets. The venture capital company is asking for a bank overdraft of £500,000 to be put in place to meet working capital needs, and is agreeable to this facility being given priority in the security arrangements.

You have links with the venture capital company, which has asked you whether you are interested in providing the overdraft. It has provided you with financial figures that the company has produced in relation to the deal.

TNC LIMITED
BALANCE SHEETS

Year ended 31 January		Audited			Projected	
	Year A £m	Year B £m	Year C £m	Year D £m	Year E £m	Year F £m
Fixed assets*	1.3	1.3	1.3	1.2	1.3	1.5
Stock	2.2	2.~	1.6	2.1	2.4	3.0
Debtors	0.3	0.3	0.3	0.3	04	04
Cash	0.1	0.2	0.4	0.5	0.5	1.3
Creditors less than one year	(2.6)	(3.0)	(2.7)	(2.6)	(3.1)	(4.0)
Net current assets	0.0	(0.3)	(0.4)	0.3	0.2	0.7
Creditors more than one year	(0.3)	(0.2)	(0.1)	-	-	(0.1)
Net assets	1.0	0.8	0.8	1.5	1.5	1.8

* Fixed assets are principally leases and improvements, which are depreciated over 10 years.

PROFIT AND LOSS SUMMARY

Year ended 31 January:	Year A £m	Audited Year B £m	Year C £m	Year D £m	Projected Year E £m	Year F £m
Sales	17.0	17.2	17.3	17.6	19.5	24.5
Gross profit	5.3	5.5	5.6	5.8	6.5	8.2
GP %	31.3%	31.9%	32.5%	32.8%	33.3%	33.5
Store direct cost	(2.1)	(2.2)	(2.2)	(2.2)	(2.5)	(3.2
Stock loss*	(0.2)	(0.2)	(0.2)	(0.2)	(0.2)	(0.2
Store fixed cost	(1.8)	(2.0)	(2.1)	(2.0)	(2.0)	(2.6)
Store contribution	1.2	1.1	1.1	1.4	1.8	2.2
Contribution %	7.1%	6.4%	6.4%	8.0%	9.2%	9.0
HQ costs	(1.1)	(1.3)	(1.0)	(1.4)	(1.5)	(1.5)
Profit before interest and tax	0.1	(0.2)	0.1	0.0	0.3	0.6
Profit before interest and tax %	0.5%	- 1.3%	0.5%	–	1.5%	2.4
Interest	(0.1)	(0.1)	(0.1)	–	(0.1)	(0.1)
Refinance fees	–	–	–	(0.1)		
Profit before tax	0.0	(0.3)	0.0	(0.1)	0.2	0.5
Profit before tax %	–	- 1.7%	–	-0.6%	1.0%	2.0
Tax	–	–	–	–	(0.1)	(0.2)
Profit after tax	0.0	(0.3)	0.0	(0.1)	0.1	0.3
Store closure provision	–	–	(0.1)	–	–	–
Retained profit	0.0	(0.3)	(0.1)	(0.1)	0.1	0.3
Sales growth (% pa)	4.6%	1.2%	0.6%	1.7%	10.8%	25.6
New store openings (closures) - number	–	–	(8)	–	2	7

* Theft, etc.

CASH FLOW SUMMARY

Year ended 31 January	Year A £m	Audited Year B £m	Year C £m	Year D £m	Projected Year E £m	Year F £m
Profit before interest and tax	0.1	(0.2)	0.1	–	0.3	0.6
Depreciation	0.2	0.2	0.1	0.2	0.1	0.2
	0.3	–	0.2	0.2	0.4	0.8
(Increase) Decrease in working capital	(0.4)	0.4	0.1	(0.4)	(0.1)	(0.2)
Interest	–	–	(0.1)	–	(0.1)	(0.1)
Tax	(0.1)	(0.1)	–	–	–	(0.1)
Cash generated by operations	(0.2)	0.3	0.2	(0.2)	0.2	0.4
Capital injection	–	–	0.1	0.5	–	0.4
Capital expenditure	(0.1)	(0.3)	(0.1)	(0.1)	(0.2)	(0.4)
Refinance fees	–	–	–	(0.1)	–	–
HP/leases	–	0.1	~			
Net cash flow	(0.3)	0.1	0.2	0.1	–	0.4

ACCOUNTING RATIOS

Year ended 31 January	Year A	Audited Year B	Year C	Year D	Projected Year E	Year F
Current ratio	1:1	0.9:1	0.9:1	1.1:1	1.1:1	1.2:1
Acid test	0.2:1	0.2:1	0.3:1	0.3:1	0.3:1	0.4:1
Net gearing (%)	20	–	–	–	–	
Credit given (days)	6	6	6	6	7	6
Credit taken (days)	81	94	84	80	87	90
Stock turnover (days)	67	67	50	65	67	67
Interest cover (times)	1.0	–	1.0	–	3.0	6.0

This business is new to the bank, so despite the introduction, caution is necessary, particularly because the company is under new management, and so its track record may not be a good guide to future performance.

In fact the company's recent performance has been poor, suggesting that there is a need for a change of course. Goode has a clear strategy for the future, which involves change. He has experience of the retail business, although one might question how relevant some of this might be to the smaller end of the market.

The bank needs to know more about the other management of the company. This is a business requiring close and detailed management control, as evidenced by the fact that 'stock loss' is a major cost.

Goode's injection of £100,000 is a sign of confidence, and the fact that he has a venture capital house interested is also positive. The company's size should enable it to secure lower prices and better credit terms from suppliers than are available to its smaller competitors. But the move into larger stores will also bring the company into greater competition with the multiple chains, which are considerably stronger.

The maintenance of sales despite the shop closures is an endorsement of the new strategy and/or Goode's skills. The projections indicate a certain degree of caution in Goode's approach – the new shops are opened in the longer term rather than immediately.

The venture capital company's plan is phased apparently in accordance with the business plan, but there will probably be performance conditions attached to the future loan stock injection. What happens if these are not met and the injection is not forthcoming?

It is interesting to see that the company's financial year ends on 31 January, which in a business like this, with a seasonal aspect to it, is likely to be the low point of the working capital cycle. The projections do not indicate a working capital borrowing requirement, but this may be hidden by the financial year-end.

Gearing is likely to be acceptable – borrowing £500,000 compared with capital of £1.5 million in the first two years. Moreover, the assumptions in relation to the main drivers of working capital need – stock turnover and credit taken – do not look unreasonable in relation to past performance.

However, historic profitability has been poor, and it is not expected to produce profit retentions until sales rise significantly in two years' time in Year E. On top of this, the Year E profit will not be there at all unless gross margin can be increased. At historic levels of gross margin, the business would be in loss in Year E and only marginally profitable in Year F, when turnover is projected to have increased significantly. The projections for profit look questionable.

The security available needs to be examined. In this kind of business a debenture is of limited value in a break-up. Debtors will be small, and premises on short leases will be subject to bankruptcy clauses. The big asset – stock – is likely to be subject to reservation of title clauses and/or rank behind heavy preferential creditors, particularly VAT, which is likely to be a very substantial liability. A receiver would have to sell the business as a going concern to produce any real value. This might not be easy given that two different management teams would have failed to make it work.

There is good income to be earned from this type of business. There will be a substantial amount of money transmission income, which will be attractive to a bank. But the sales increase and required gross margin improvements look too demanding in what is a very competitive marketplace. If the overdraft facility is ever heavily utilised, it will mean something has gone wrong.

The new concept is unproven, and on balance the business looks too risky. An alternative for the bank would be to suggest that, in view of the absence of an overdraft requirement in Year D, the account would be taken on a credit basis and the possibility of lending to the company considered later in the light of a longer track record under the new management.

13

Clubs and associations

Lending propositions for unincorporated clubs and associations are relatively rare, but can be awkward for a banker to deal with. The propositions are rare because a club is not an ordinary business in the sense that its activities are directed to making a profit. It is, rather, a collection of individuals who get together for some common – usually essentially social – purpose. While a club may trade – for example, it will often have a bar-trading will be ancillary to its main purpose. If individual members decide to leave, they can do so quite easily simply by resigning or not renewing their subscriptions; they are not shareholders who cannot easily get their capital out of a limited company, or partners or sole traders who will be personally liable for the debts of their businesses.

So a great deal of circumspection is needed when lending to an unincorporated club or association. More than in the case of an ordinary business, club members should take full responsibility for providing the capital needed to run the club. In these circumstances borrowing should be rare, and this is particularly true of borrowing for working capital purposes. Clubs ought not to have debtors to be financed. Their services are predominantly sold to members, who should pay cash on delivery or in advance.

There can, for example, be no justification for borrowing in anticipation of subscription income to meet short-term debts. Clubs will have some stock, for example drink, cigarettes, and so on for a bar, but breweries are generally prepared to offer generous credit terms to clubs, and there is usually a good prospect of stock's being financed by brewery creditors. All in all, it is a poorly organized club that cannot provide funds to meet working capital needs without borrowing from outside. So as far as a bank is concerned, club bank accounts should normally run in credit and any borrowing propositions ought to be only for major capital expenditure purposes.

Club management

This is the first awkward problem that arises when dealing with many clubs. The management of most clubs is in the hands of members. Few clubs have professional managers, and the equivalent of a company's board of directors is the club committee. While individual committee members may specialize in terms of function – for example, a club treasurer will look after finance and may be functionally well qualified (the treasurer of a club is very often an accountant) the committee members are normally part-time and unpaid. They cannot therefore be expected to give the same priority to their club work as they would to their own employment or business activities. This is a very broad generalization, as there are many clubs that are professionally run by their 'amateur' managers, and there are also many club committee members who show an unusual degree of dedication to their function.

However, as a generality a lender must not expect club 'management' to be anything other than of variable quality. Club committees will often look at things through 'rose tinted spectacles', and will find it hard to be objective when dealing with people who are their friends. They can, for example, often be very naïve and unbusinesslike over the handling of cash. Any good publican knows how important it is to control tightly the activities of barmen and women to ensure that cash takings do not 'leak'. Defalcations by club barmen are a perennial problem. Particularly in the case of clubs where the bar is manned by the members themselves, it is hard for club 'managers' to find that their trust can sometimes be misplaced. The capacity of a club to maintain a reasonable gross profit margin on its bar activities is often a very good test of the professionalism of its day-to-day management.

The fact that club management may be unprofessional can lead them to have over-optimistic (and at worst, unrealistic) expectations of their capacity to repay any proposed borrowing. Club committee members may well be influential individuals in a community, and may also be important personal or even business customers of a bank in their own right. The pressures on a lender to agree to what the club wants may therefore be considerable. Where influential people are concerned these pressures cannot realistically be ignored, but the lender must stick to his or her guns and insist on a full appraisal of a proposition backed by all the necessary projections. If a club committee is acting in an amateurish way, it is all the more important for a banker to inject the necessary professionalism.

Legal issues

Unlike limited companies, clubs and associations are not separate legal entities. They do not have powers to enter into contracts and cannot be sued for their debts. Individual members are not normally personally liable for any debts undertaken by the club officers, and despite there being legal precedent to indicate that committee members could be personally liable, the position is by no means clear.

The lender will want to ensure that someone with a legal responsibility to repay a borrowing assumes full liability. The lending should be made either on a separate account in the names of the responsible club officers or in the name of the club itself, supported by appropriate guarantees. The borrowing must conform with any formalities and restrictions laid down in the club rules, and these will need to be checked for this purpose.

The financial statements produced by many clubs are often rudimentary, and need to be treated with care. They may well be produced by an amateur at accounting, and they do not have to be audited, although they usually are. However, the auditor will usually be unpaid and will be an amateur him or herself. Very often, the auditor will be another club member, so the financial statements are open to the possibility of being inaccurate or misleading, even if this is by accident. The lender therefore needs to be healthily sceptical when looking at the figures.

Security matters

Unincorporated clubs and associations cannot own property. If a lending is required for the acquisition of, or to be secured by a charge over, property, this will have to be held by trustees on behalf of the club. The club's rules will need to contain provision for property to be held by nominated trustees and cover their powers to charge the property as security. A trust deed must be drawn up covering the powers of the trustees. Trustees have no implied power to charge trust assets so they need to be authorized to do so under the terms of the trust. Lending to trustees has to be made on loan account when secured by trust property.

A more common security for clubs and associations is simply by taking personal guarantees from committee members. For any substantial borrowing, these guarantees need to be backed by tangible security, which will often be a second mortgage on the individual's house. The interest of spouses in the matrimonial home must be fully taken into account, and it is particularly important that they have independent legal advice before committing themselves to a charge.

Case 1

Womblefield Lawn Tennis Club has banked with your branch for over 20 years, maintaining current and deposit accounts, the present balances of which total £6,000. The club, which has 100 members, does not own its own tennis courts, but operates on four municipal courts hired for fixed periods each week from the local authority. Near to the courts the club has a prefabricated wooden pavilion, which it uses as changing rooms.

For some years membership has been static. There are many other tennis clubs in the area, and Womblefield's poor facilities have made it unfashionable. A high proportion of members are young people of school age, who are attracted by the low membership subscriptions. The club committee have been seeking an alternative site for some time, and a local farmer has now agreed to provide sufficient land to build six tennis courts, a car park and club house on a 50-year lease at a nominal rent, on the basis that the property will revert to him if tennis is not played there regularly. The local authority has given an indication that it would be willing to grant planning permission for sports facilities on the site. The cost of transforming it has been estimated at £40,000 for six tennis courts including floodlighting, £12,000 for installing utilities and roadworks, and £48,000 to build a club house.

The Lawn Tennis Association has indicated that it would provide a grant of £15,000 towards the cost of the courts. The club's present pavilion can be dismantled and sold at an estimated price of £2,000. The grant will be available immediately the courts have been completed.

The club chairman, Harold Walker, treasurer, Desmond Runner, and secretary, Michael Sprinter, call to see you. They are all longstanding personal customers of your branch, and you are aware that they have equities in their houses of £30,000, £25,000 and £20,000 respectively. Runner and Sprinter are in their mid-40s with teenage families, while Walker is a bachelor aged 60. Walker has retired early with a good pension, and in addition has £20,000 on deposit with you, which he says he is prepared to advance to the club as an interest-free loan.

Runner has produced projections of future income at the new site. His figures are as follows:

	Year 1 £	Year 2 £	Year 3 £	Year 4 £	Year 5 £
Membership	150	200	250	300	300
Subscriptions	7,500	10,400	13,750	17,400	18,300
Sponsorship/ social events	2,000	2,500	3,000	3,000	3,000
Bar profits	1,500	2,000	2,500	3,000	3,000
Tournaments	450	600	750	900	900
Total income	11,450	15,500	20,000	24,300	25,200

Walker asks you for a loan of £57,000 over 15 years. On consulting your repayment tables you find that the monthly repayments of principal and interest for such a loan, at the rate you would expect to charge, amount to £12 for each £1,000 borrowed.

WOMBLEFIELD LAWN TENNIS CLUB

As at 30 September Receipts	Year A £	Year B £	Year C £	Payments	Year A £	Year B £	Year C £
Subscriptions	3,643	4,079	4,727	Court hire	2,631	2,530	2,234
Tournament fees	418	325	256	Rates	33	35	45
Disco profit	89	29	171	Balls	392	494	770
Interest	344	339	407	Tournament expenses	64	3	12
Legacy	–	1,200	–	Trophies	139	299	182
				Coaching	160	200	200
				County LTA affiliation fees	177	284	274
				Insurance	84	125	135
				Pavilion maintenance	149	106	134
				Printing, stationery, telephone, etc.	221	77	183
				Sundries	610	502	94
					4,660	4,655	4,263
	4,494	5,972	5,561	Closing bank C/A and D/A	4,057	5,374	6,672
Bank opening C/A and D/A	4,223	4,057	5,374		8,717	10,029	10,935
	8,717	10,029	10,935				

233

This proposition is not an untypical club lending request. It is surrounded by a degree of naive optimism, but within the request there is the possibility of agreeing a more modest proposal. The club committee will have to be led to this conclusion, however, by the professionalism of the lender.

All the indications are that this club is run by amateurs, so a high quality of management information could not be expected. The first thing to be looked at sceptically must be the amount requested. Is it correct? The basic figures are:

	£	£
Cost		100,000
Less present balance	6,000	
Sale of pavilion	2,000	
LTA grant	15,000	
Interest-free loan	20,000	43,000
		57,000

But this is not enough. What about legal costs and fixtures and fittings? There is going to be a bar stock so there may be a need for working capital. Overall, it is likely that the true amount needed would be nearer to £65,000 rather than £57,000, which, on the figures given, would suggest annual loan repayments of around £9,500.

The projections produced are very amateurish too. There are no figures given for expenses at the new site. One obvious potential increase is the amount that the local authority would charge for rates on the new building. Against this, court hire will disappear as an expense, which will save something over £2,000 per annum.

Overall, the projections look far too optimistic, and they cannot be taken at face value. The plans for the future need to be tested against past performance. It is important to look at the historic annual cash-generating capacity of the club, which has been as follows:

	Year A £	Year B £	Year C £
Closing balance	4,057	5,374	6,672
Less: Opening balance	4,223	4,057	5,374
	(166)	1,317	1,298
Less: Interest received	344	339	407
Legacy	–	1,200	–
	(510)	(222)	891

Taking last year:

	£
Cash surplus	891
Add: Court hire	2,234
	3,125

The underlying cash generation of the club is improving and, based on Year C's performance, annual payments of something around £3,000 would appear to be more feasible than the required £9,500, although this assumes that increased income will cover increased expenditure of the new site.

The key issues will be: How quickly will membership increase at the new site, and how quickly can subscriptions be raized? Is the new site as convenient as the present one for existing members? Can other fundraising activities be as successful as indicated? A fair degree of probing will be needed to establish reasonably conservative estimates of future income from these items.

The lease of the new site would have very little value as security because the land will revert to the freeholder if the venture is unsuccessful, which would be when the security would be needed. Guarantees from the club officials supported by the equities in their houses might provide adequate security, but in practice this would be a dubious proposition. As presented, the lending request is highly speculative, and it is difficult to see how independent legal advice to the wives of the club officials will allow them to put their homes at serious risk for the sake of their husbands' involvement in a tennis club!

Given the speculative nature of the proposition and the lack of adequate security, the lending request has to be declined. However, there is a way of re-engineering the proposition to make it into a possible agreement. The club and its officials are longstanding customers, and most lenders would like to give some sort of agreement rather than just send these important people away. The main problem with the request is the cost of the new club building, but if the existing pavilion were transferred initially to the new site, the whole arrangement would become much more manageable. The borrowing requirement would be cut by approximately £46,000, leaving a borrowing requirement of £19,000, which it looks feasible for the club to repay. If the club can subsequently demonstrate that it can achieve its income projections, then the possibility of building a new and more expensive clubhouse could be considered in the future.

Case 2

Twickendon Rugby Club was founded over 30 years ago, and has banked with your branch throughout its existence. Its accounts have always been maintained in credit. The club occupies an eight-acre site in an area that was once open country but which is now an up-market housing estate. Its first president, Mr Andrew Johnson, granted the club a 45-year lease on the land at a fixed rent of £500 p.a. Johnson died recently. In his will he has given the club an option to buy the freehold of the site for £100,000. This option has to be exercized within 12 months of Johnson's death.

The club's current president, Angus Wilkins, and its treasurer, David Taylor, call to see you. They tell you that the club would like to buy the land, and ask whether the bank would be prepared to lend it the £100,000 needed.

Taylor is a partner in a reputable firm of local estate agents. He tells you that, in his opinion, there is a good chance that the club would get planning permission to build houses on the land, which he believes would then conservatively be worth £100,000 per acre. The club's intention would be to sell the land to a builder after obtaining planning permission, and relocate to a cheaper site outside the town.

The bank would be offered a charge over the land, and would be repaid as soon as the sale could be completed. Wilkins and Taylor have brought with them the club's latest accounts.

This proposition concerns what may be a quite unique opportunity for a not-very-well-run club to put itself on a sound financial basis. However, the approach of the club officials to the opportunity is naïve.

An analysis of the recent financial statements shows that the club is in some difficulty and is not particularly well managed. The core income – subscriptions – is falling steadily, suggesting quite an alarming drop in membership. This is having a knock-on effect in other areas: for example, donations from members (in practice members' loans to the club being written off) reducing in Year C. Income from social activities has held up, but there is no great evidence of any energetic fundraising although, given the cash drain seen, this is essential for the future well-being of the club.

Bar takings are erratic, and have declined since Year A in line with the fall in membership. However, the really damning feature of the management is the inconsistent and, from Year B to Year C, significant decline in the bar profit percentage from 28% to 20.7%. In a club like this it is vital that cash and bar sales are tightly controlled, and this has clearly not happened. Given that there is no reason to reduce bar prices, the decline has to be due to either one or a combination of cash leakage, poor stock control or failure to pass on price rises to members. It can be seen that if the 28% margin had been maintained, there would have been £1,760 more income to reduce the net loss – a big figure for this club.

The net profit percentage shows that ignoring extraordinary items – and the fact that there appears to have been a botch in the payment of VAT is another warning sign – the overall deterioration is getting worse. The decline in the current ratio and acid test figures shows a steadily worsening liquidity position. The cash haemorrhage cannot be allowed to continue for much longer, as in 12 months or so, on present trends, the club will need to borrow to meet operating expenses, and this will be clearly unacceptable.

The only positive thing that can be said about the financial statements is that the net worth of the club is probably understated, as the lease of the land is not given a value in the balance sheet. It must be worth something and might be very valuable, if Taylor's views on the development potential of the site are correct.

The presentation of the proposition is amateurish. The officials are only asking for the bare £100,000, and no account seems to have been taken of expenses and so on, which the club has no cash resources of its own to meet. Fundamentally it is speculative, as

TWICKENDON RUGBY CLUB
BALANCE SHEET

As at 30 April	Year A £	£	Year B £	£	Year C £	£
Fixed assets						
Clubhouse and car park	22,931		22,359		21,787	
Floodlights	5,173		4,139		3,009	
Fixtures and fittings	2,038		4,768		4,234	
Training equipment	1,126	31,268	750	32,016	376	29,406
Current assets						
Cash	12,569		3,628		1,787	
Debtors	777		1,538		613	
Stock (bar and kit)	910		2,869		2,388	
	14,256		8,035		4,788	
Less: Current liabilities						
Creditors	(3,638)		(4,941)		(3,357)	
Net current assets		10,618		3,094		1,431
Less: Loans (interest free)						
Members	6,320		4,240		3,700	
Brewery	9,921	(16,241)	9,706	(13,946)	9,477	(13,177)
		25,645		21,164		17,660
Financed by:						
Accumulated fund	25,786		25,645		21,164	
Profit/loss for the year	(141)	25,645	(4,481)	21,164	(3,504)	17,660

RATIOS AND OTHER INFORMATION

	Year A	Year B	Year C
Bar profit (%)	24.3	28.0	20.7
Net profit (loss) (%)	(0.8)	(10.9)	(27.8)
Current ratio	3.9:1	1.6:1	1.4:1
Acid test	3.7:1	1:1	0.7:1

INCOME AND EXPENDITURE ACCOUNT

Year to 30 April	Year A		Year B		Year C	
	£	£	£	£	£	£
Membership						
Donations	3,293		3,901		2,480	
Subscriptions	4,011	7,304	3,718	7,619	2,773	5,253
Bar account						
Opening stock	1,128		678		966	
Purchases	20,506		15,834		19,125	
	21,634		16,512		20,091	
Closing stock	(678)		(966)		(903)	
Cost of sales	20,956		15,546		19,188	
Bar takings	27,672	6,716	21,579	6,033	24,206	5,018
Club activities						
Social events	731		433		1,220	
Raffles	1,058		1,632		953	
Interest	118	1,907	223	2,288	141	2,314
Total income		15,927		15,940		12,585
Expenditure						
Playing expenditure	1,473		1,653		2,295	
Rates	1,451		1,195		1,530	
Heat and light	1,913		2,638		2,029	
Insurance	929		1,118		1,222	
Telephone	369		63		394	
Repairs and renewals	4,344		4,999		2,735	
Rent	500		500		500	
Groundsman	–		335		170	
Postage and printing	384		483		273	
Depreciation	2,017		2,516		2,610	
Interest	91		75		124	
Sundry expenses	2,597	16,068	2,095	17,670	2,207	16,089
Profit/(Loss)		(141)		(1,730)		(3,504)
Extraordinary item (VAT assessment re prior years)		–		(2,751)		
Total income		(141)		(4,481)		(3,504)

there is no guarantee that planning permission on the land will be granted. As a banking proposition it could only be undertaken if there was a satisfactory fall-back position under which the club could demonstrate that it could repay the borrowing over, say, a 10-year term. This it patently cannot do on recent performance. Even if planning permission were certain, the club could not meet interest pending on the sale of the land.

The security position is also dubious. The land without planning permission will be difficult to value. Will it really be worth £100,000 without planning permission? If the local authority declined the planning application and insisted it remained a sports field it could be worth a fairly negligible amount. No prudent banker would place reliance on the 'hope value' of £100,000 per acre with the benefit of planning permission.

The response to the proposition has to be an emphatic no. The way forward would be for the officials to apply for and obtain planning permission while simultaneously looking for a buyer for the land. Some sort of closed bridge might then be possible, but this is as far as a bank would wish to go.

Index

Advances against bills held for
    collection 184
Avalising 186

Bills negotiated 184
Building advance cash
    flow forecastlng 81
Building as an ordinary business 80

Capital expenditure, definition 55
Capital Expenditure/Depreciation 58
Capital investment appraisal 55
Cash flow analysis – debt
    service relationship 202
Club management 228
Construction Risk 108
Control 198
Control of cash 150

Disposal Risk 108
Documentary Credit Facilities 186

Exchange risk 187, 198
Export finance 183
Financial accounts, Historical 2
Financial risks 150
Financial statements 127
Forfaiting 185

Import finance 185

Legal and accounting issues 110
Legal issues 229

Management accounts 4
Management issues 149
Management stake 204
Marginal Risk 187
Mezzanine debt 200

Operating Cash Flow 58
Ordinary shares 199
Overtradlng 24

Personal financial phllosophy 12
Physical delivery 198
Portion control 149
Preference shares 200
Professional approach 2
Property development 100
Property investment 97
Property investment transaction. 104
Protection against downside risk 169

Quality 198
Quality of management 126

Rationale for the structure 201

Security 128
Security matters 229
Senior debt 200
Senior debt capacity 202
Serviceability 168
Settlement Risk 187
Standards of hygiene 150
Structuring the financing 199
Sustainable cash flow 56

The value of secondary exits 203
Types of property transaction 97

Undertrading 26

Working Capital Variation 57
Working capital, concept 23